A Little Java, A Few Patterns

A Little Java, A Few Patterns

Matthias Felleisen

Rice University
Houston, Texas

Daniel P. Friedman

Indiana University
Bloomington, Indiana

Drawings by Duane Bibby

Foreword by Ralph E. Johnson

The MIT Press
Cambridge, Massachusetts
London, England

This book was set by the authors and was printed and bound in the United States of America.

Library of Congress Cataloging-in-Publication Data

Felleisen, Matthias
   A little Java, a few patterns. / Matthias Felleisen and Daniel P. Friedman; drawings by Duane Bibby; foreword by Ralph E. Johnson
     p.   cm.
  Includes index and bibliographical references.
  ISBN 0-262-56115-8 (pbk : alk. paper)
  1. Java (Computer program language) I. Friedman, Daniel P. II. Title.
QA76.73.J38F45   1998
005.13′3—dc21   97-40548
                                                                  CIP

To Helga, Christopher, and Sebastian.
To Mary, Rob, Rachel, Sara,
and to the memory of Brian.

Contents

FOREWORD

Learning to program is more than learning the syntactic and semantic rules of a programming language. It also requires learning how to *design* programs. Any good book on programming must therefore teach program design.

Like any other form of design, program design has competing schools. These schools are often associated with a particular set of languages. Since Java is an object-oriented programming language, people teaching Java should emphasize object-oriented design.

Felleisen and Friedman show that the functional (input-output driven) method of program design naturally leads to the use of well-known object-oriented design patterns. In fact, they integrate the two styles seamlessly and show how well they work together. Their book proves that the functional design method does not clash with, but supports object-oriented programming.

Their success doesn't surprise me, because I've seen it in Smalltalk for many years, though unfortunately, it seems to have remained one of the secrets of object-oriented design. I am happy to see that Felleisen and Friedman have finally exposed it. This book will be especially useful if you are a C++ programmer learning Java, since you probably haven't seen functional program design before. If you know functional design, the book will gently introduce you to pattern-based programming in Java. If you don't know it, Felleisen and Friedman will teach you a powerful new way of thinking that you should add to your design toolbox.

Enjoy the pizzas!

Ralph E. Johnson
Champaign, Illinois

Preface

An object-oriented programming language enables a programmer to construct reusable program components. With such components, other programmers can quickly build large new programs and program fragments. In the ideal case, the programmers do not modify any existing code but simply glue together components and add a few new ones. This reusability of components, however, does not come for free. It requires a well-designed object-oriented language and a strict discipline of programming.

Java is a such a language, and this book introduces its object-oriented elements: (abstract) classes, fields, methods, inheritance, and interfaces. This small core language has a simple semantic model, which greatly helps programmers to express themselves. In addition, Java implementations automatically manage the memory a program uses, which frees programmers from thinking about machine details and encourages them to focus on design.

The book's second goal is to introduce the reader to design patterns, the key elements of a programming discipline that enhances code reuse. Design patterns help programmers organize their object-oriented components so that they properly implement the desired computational process. More importantly still, design patterns help communicate important properties about a program component. If a component is an instance of an explicitly formulated pattern and documented as such, other programmers can easily understand its structure and reuse it in their own programs, even without access to the component's source.

THE INTENDED AUDIENCE

The book is primarily intended for people—practicing programmers, instructors and students alike—who wish to study the essential elements of object-oriented programming and the idea of design patterns. Readers must have some basic programming experience. They will benefit most from the book if they understand the principles of functional design, that is, the design of program fragments based on their input-output behavior. An introductory computer science course that uses Scheme (or ML) is the best way to get familiar with this style of design, but it is not required.

WHAT THIS BOOK IS NOT ABOUT

Java provides many useful features and libraries beyond its object-oriented core. While these additional Java elements are important for professional programming, their coverage would distract from the book's important goals: object-oriented programming and the use of design patterns. For that reason, this book is not a complete introduction to Java. Still, readers who master its contents can quickly become skilled Java programmers with the supplementary sources listed in the *Commencement*.

The literature on design patterns evolves quickly. Thus, there is quite a bit more to patterns than an introductory book could intelligibly cover. Yet, the simplicity of the patterns we use and the power that they provide should encourage readers to study the additional references about patterns mentioned at the end of the book.

ACKNOWLEDGMENTS

We are indebted to many people for their contributions and assistance throughout the development of this book. Several extensive discussions with Shriram Krishnamurthi, Jon Rossie, and Mitch Wand kept us on track; their detailed comments deeply influenced our thinking at critical junctures. Michael Ashley, Sundar Balasubramaniam, Cynthia Brown, Peter Drake, Bob Filman, Robby Findler, Steve Ganz, Paul Graunke, John Greiner, Erik Hilsdale, Matthew Kudzin, Julia Lawall, Shinn-Der Lee, Michael Levin, Gary McGraw, Benjamin Pierce, Amr Sabry, Jonathan Sobel, and George Springer read the book at various stages of development and their comments helped produce the final result. We also wish to thank Robert Prior at MIT Press who loyally supported us for many years and fostered the idea of a "Little Java." The book greatly benefited from Dorai Sitaram's incredibly clever Scheme typesetting program SLATEX. Finally, we would like to thank the National Science Foundation for its continued support and especially for the Educational Innovation Grant that provided us with the opportunity to collaborate for the past year.

READING GUIDELINES

Do not rush through this book. Allow seven sittings, at least. Read carefully. Mark up the book or take notes; valuable hints are scattered throughout the text. Work through the examples, don't scan them. Keep in mind the motto "Think first, experiment later."

The book is a dialogue about interesting Java programs. After you have understood the examples, experiment with them, that is, modify the programs and examples and see how they behave. Since most Java implementations are unfortunately batch interpreters or compilers, this requires work of a repetitive nature on your side. Some hints on how to experiment with Java are provided on the following pages.

We do not give any formal definitions in this book. We believe that you can form your own definitions and thus remember and understand them better than if we had written them out for you. But be sure you know and understand the bits of advice that appear in most chapters.

We use a few notational conventions throughout the text to help you understand the programs on several levels. The primary conventions concern typeface for different kinds of words. Field and method names are in *italic*. Basic data, including numbers, booleans, and constructors introduced via datatypes are set in sans serif. Keywords, e.g., **class**, **abstract**, **return** and **interface** are in **boldface**. When you experiment, you may ignore the typefaces but not the related framenotes. To highlight this role of typefaces, the programs in framenotes are set in a `typewriter` face.

Food appears in many of our examples for two reasons. First, food is easier to visualize than abstract ideas. (This is not a good book to read while dieting.) We hope the choice of food will help you understand the examples and concepts we use. Second, we want to provide you with a little distraction. We know how frustrating the subject matter can be, and a little distraction will help you keep your sanity.

You are now ready to start. Good luck! We hope you will enjoy the experiences waiting for you on the following pages.

Bon appétit!

Matthias Felleisen
Daniel P. Friedman

Experimenting with Java

Here are some hints on how to experiment with Java:[1]

1. Create a file that contains a complete hierarchy of classes.

2. To each class whose name does *not* end with a superscript $\mathcal{D}$, $\mathcal{V}$, $\mathcal{I}$, or $\mathcal{M}$, add a toString method according to these rules:

   a) if the class does not contain any fields, use

```
public String toString() {
  return "new " + getClass().getName() + "()"; }
```

   b) if the class has one field, say x, use

```
public String toString() {
  return "new " + getClass().getName() + "(" + x + ")"; }
```

   c) if the class has two fields, say x and y, use

```
public String toString() {
  return "new " + getClass().getName() + "(" + x + ", " + y + ")"; }
```

3. Add the following class at the bottom of the file:

```
class Main {
 public static void main(String args[ ]) {
   DataType_or_Interface y = new _ _ _ _ _;
   System.out.println( ...... ); } }
```

With DataType_or_Interface y = new _ _ _ _ _, create the object y with which you wish to experiment. Then replace ...... with the example expression that you would like to experiment with. For example, if you wish to experiment with the distanceTo0 method of ManhattanPt as defined in chapter 2, add the following definition to the end of your file:

```
class Main {
 public static void main(String args[ ]) {
   PointD y = new ManhattanPt(2,8);
   System.out.println( y.distanceTo0() ); } }
```

---

[1] See Arnold and Gosling [1] for details on how they work. These hints make little sense out of context, so for now, just follow them as you read this book.

If you wish to experiment with a sequence of expressions that modify y, as in chapter 10, *e.g.*,

```
y._ _ _ _ _ _ ;
y._ _ _ _ _ _ ;
y._ _ _ _ _ _
```

replace ...... with

```
y._ _ _ _ _ _ _ + "\n " +
y._ _ _ _ _ _ _ + "\n " +
y._ _ _ _ _ _
```

For example, if you wish to experiment with the methods of `PiemanM` as defined in chapter 10, add the following definition to the end of your file:

```
class Main {
 public static void main(String args[ ]) {
  PiemanI y = new PiemanM();
  System.out.println(
   y.addTop(new Anchovy()) + "\n" +
   y.addTop(new Anchovy()) + "\n" +
   y.substTop(new Tuna(),new Anchovy()) ); } }
```

4. Finally, compile the file and interpret the class `Main`.

A Little Java, A Few Patterns

1.
Modern Toys

Is **5** an integer?	[1] Yes, it is.
Is this a number: −23?	[2] Yes, but we don't use negative integers.
Is this an integer: 5.32?	[3] No, and we don't use this type of number.
What type of number is 5?	[4] **int**.[1] [1] In Java, **int** stands for "integer."
Quick, think of another integer!	[5] How about 19?
What type of value is true?	[6] **boolean**.
What type of value is false?	[7] **boolean**.
Can you think of another **boolean**?	[8] No, that's all there is to **boolean**.
What is **int**?	[9] A type.
What is **boolean**?	[10] Another type.
What is a type?	[11] A type is a name for a collection of values.
What is a type?	[12] Sometimes we use it as if it were the collection.
Can we make new types?	[13] We don't know how yet.

Draw the picture that characterizes the essential relationships among the following classes.

abstract class Seasoning$^{\mathcal{D}}$ {}

class Salt **extends** Seasoning$^{\mathcal{D}}$ {}

class Pepper **extends** Seasoning$^{\mathcal{D}}$ {}

$^{\mathcal{D}}$ This superscript is a reminder that the class is a datatype. Lower superscripts when you enter this kind of definition in a file: `SeasoningD`.

14 Is this it?

Yes. We say Seasoning$^{\mathcal{D}}$ is a datatype, and Salt and Pepper are its variants.

15 Okay. But aren't all three classes introducing new types?

Yes, in a way. Now, is

   new Salt()

a Seasoning$^{\mathcal{D}}$?

16 Yes, it is, because **new** Salt() creates an instance of Salt, and every instance of Salt is also a Seasoning$^{\mathcal{D}}$.

And

   new Pepper()?

17 It's also a Seasoning$^{\mathcal{D}}$, because **new** Pepper() creates an instance of Pepper, and every instance of Pepper is also a Seasoning$^{\mathcal{D}}$.

What are **abstract**, **class**, and **extends**?

18 Easy:
   abstract class introduces a datatype,
   class introduces a variant, and
   extends connects a variant to a datatype.

Is there any other Seasoning$^{\mathcal{D}}$?

19 No, because only Salt and Pepper extend Seasoning$^{\mathcal{D}}$.[1]

---

[1] Evaluating `new Salt()` twice does not produce the same value, but we ignore the distinction for now.

Correct, **Salt** and **Pepper** are the only variants of the datatype $Seasoning^{\mathcal{D}}$. Have we seen a datatype like $Seasoning^{\mathcal{D}}$ before?

[20] No, but **boolean** is a type that also has just two values.

Let's define more $Seasoning^{\mathcal{D}}$s.

[21]

```
class Thyme extends Seasoning𝒟 {}
```

We can have lots of $Seasoning^{\mathcal{D}}$s.

```
class Sage extends Seasoning𝒟 {}
```

And then there were four.

[22] Yes.

What is a Cartesian point?

[23] It is basically a pair of numbers.

What is a point in Manhattan?

[24] An intersection where two city streets meet.

How do **CartesianPt** and **ManhattanPt** differ from **Salt** and **Pepper**?

[25] Each of them contains three things between { and }. The x and the y are obviously the coordinates of the points. But what is the remaining thing above the bold bar?[1]

```
abstract class Point𝒟 {}
```

```
class CartesianPt extends Point𝒟 {
  int x;
  int y;
  CartesianPt(int _x,int _y) {
    x = _x;
    y = _y; }
  _____
}
```

```
class ManhattanPt extends Point𝒟 {
  int x;
  int y;
  ManhattanPt(int _x,int _y) {
    x = _x;
    y = _y; }
  _____
}
```

---

[1] This bar indicates the end of the constructor definition. It is used as an eye-catching separator. We recommend that you use
```
// ----------------------------
```
when you enter it in a file.

The underlined occurrences of CartesianPt and ManhattanPt introduce the constructors of the respective variants.

²⁶ How do we use these constructors?

A constructor is used with **new** to create new instances of a **class**.

²⁷ Obvious!

When we create a CartesianPt like this:

   new CartesianPt(2,3),

we use the constructor in the definition of CartesianPt.

²⁸ So now we have created a CartesianPt whose x field is 2 and whose y field is 3. And because CartesianPt **extends** Point$^{\mathcal{D}}$, it is also a Point$^{\mathcal{D}}$.

Correct. Is this a ManhattanPt:

   new ManhattanPt(2,3)?

²⁹ Yes, and its x field is 2 and its y field is 3.

Isn't all this obvious?

³⁰ Mostly, but that means we have used constructors before without defining them. How does that work?

When a **class** does not contain any fields, as in Salt and Pepper, a constructor is included by default.

³¹ And that's the constructor we used before, right?

Yes, that's correct. Default constructors never consume values, and, when used with **new**, always create objects without fields.

³² Good. But what is **new** Point$^{\mathcal{D}}$()?

An **abstract** class is by definition incomplete, so **new** cannot create an instance from it.

³³ That makes sense. Let's move on.

Do the following classes define another datatype with variants?

| 34 | Yes, they define a datatype and two variants. |

abstract class Num$^{\mathcal{D}}$ {}

class Zero **extends** Num$^{\mathcal{D}}$ {}

class OneMoreThan **extends** Num$^{\mathcal{D}}$ {
  Num$^{\mathcal{D}}$ *predecessor*;
  OneMoreThan(Num$^{\mathcal{D}}$ _p) {
    predecessor = _p; }

}

Draw the picture, too.

Is this a Num$^{\mathcal{D}}$:

  new Zero()?

| 35 | Obviously, just like **new** Salt() is a Seasoning$^{\mathcal{D}}$. |

Is this a Num$^{\mathcal{D}}$:
  new OneMoreThan(
    new Zero())?

| 36 | Yes, because OneMoreThan constructs a Num$^{\mathcal{D}}$ from a Num$^{\mathcal{D}}$, and every instance of OneMoreThan is also a Num$^{\mathcal{D}}$. |

How does OneMoreThan do that?

| 37 | We give it **new** Zero(), which is a Num$^{\mathcal{D}}$, and it constructs a new Num$^{\mathcal{D}}$. |

And what does it mean to construct this new instance?

| 38 | This new instance of OneMoreThan is a value with a single field, which is called *predecessor*. In our example, the field is **new** Zero(). |

Does *predecessor* always stand for an instance of Zero?

| 39 | No, its type says that it stands for a Num$^{\mathcal{D}}$, which, at the moment, may be either a Zero or a OneMoreThan. |

What is
  new OneMoreThan(
    new OneMoreThan(
      new Zero())))?
	⁴⁰ A Num$^\mathcal{D}$, because OneMoreThan constructs an instance from a Num$^\mathcal{D}$ and we agreed that
	    new OneMoreThan(
	      new Zero())
	is a Num$^\mathcal{D}$.

What is
  new OneMoreThan(
    0)?

⁴¹ That is nonsense,[1] because 0 is not a Num$^\mathcal{D}$.

_____

[1] We use the word "nonsense" to refer to expressions for which Java cannot determine a type.

Is **new** Zero() the same as 0?

⁴² No, 0 is similar to, but not the same as,
    new Zero().

Is
  new OneMoreThan(
    new Zero())
like
  1?

⁴³ 1 is similar to, but not the same as,
    new OneMoreThan(
      new Zero()).

And what is
  new OneMoreThan(
    new OneMoreThan(
      new OneMoreThan(
        new OneMoreThan(
          new Zero())))))
similar to?

⁴⁴ 4.

Are there more Num$^\mathcal{D}$s than **boolean**s?

⁴⁵ Lots.

Are there more Num$^\mathcal{D}$s than **int**s?

⁴⁶ No.[1]

_____

[1] This answer is only conceptually correct. Java limits the number of **int**s to approximately 2^{32}.

What is the difference between **new Zero()** and 0?	[47] Easy: **new Zero()** is an instance of **Zero** and, by implication, is a $\text{Num}^{\mathcal{D}}$, whereas 0 is an **int**. This makes it difficult to compare them, but we can compare them in our minds.
Correct. In general, if two things are instances of two different basic types, they cannot be the same.	[48] So are types just names for different collections with no common instances?
The primitive types (**int** and **boolean**) are distinct; others may overlap.	[49] What are non-basic types?
Class definitions do not introduce primitive types. For example, a value like **new Zero()** is not only an instance of **Zero**, but is also a $\text{Num}^{\mathcal{D}}$, which is extended by **Zero**. Indeed, it is of any type that $\text{Num}^{\mathcal{D}}$ extends, too.	[50] And what is that?
Every class that does not explicitly extend another class implicitly extends the class **Object**.	[51] This must mean that everything is an **Object**.
Almost. We will soon see what that means.	[52] Okay.

The First Bit of Advice

When specifying a collection of data, use abstract classes for datatypes and extended classes for variants.

What do the following define?

```
abstract class Layer^D {}
```

```
class Base extends Layer^D {
  Object o;
  Base(Object _o) {
    o = _o; }

}
```

```
class Slice extends Layer^D {
  Layer^D l;
  Slice(Layer^D _l) {
    l = _l; }

}
```

They define a new datatype and its two variants. The first variant contains a field of type Object.

What is
  new Base(
    new Zero())?

It looks like an instance of Base, which means it is also a Layer^D and an Object.

And what is
  new Base(
    new Salt())?

It also looks like an instance of Base. But how come both
    new Base(
      new Zero())
and
    new Base(
      new Salt())
are instances of the same variant?

They are, because everything created with **new** is an Object, the class of all objects.

Hence, we can use both
    new Zero()
and
    new Salt()
for the construction of a Base, which requires an Object.

Is anything else an Object?

57 We said that only things created with **new** are Objects.[1]

---
[1] Arrays and strings are objects, too. We don't discuss them.

Correct. Is this a Layer$^{\mathcal{D}}$:
  new Base(
    5)?

58 5 is not created with **new**, so this must be nonsense.

Is this a Layer$^{\mathcal{D}}$:
  new Base(
    false)?

59 false is not created with **new**, so this must be nonsense, too.

Correct again! How about this Layer$^{\mathcal{D}}$:
  new Base(
    new Integer(5))?

60 This must mean that Integer creates an object from an **int**.

Guess how we create a Layer$^{\mathcal{D}}$ from false?

61 Easy now:
    new Base(
      new Boolean(false)).

Is it confusing that we need to connect **int** with Integer and **boolean** with Boolean?

62 Too much coffee does that.

Ready for more?

63 Can't wait.

2.
Methods to
Our Madness

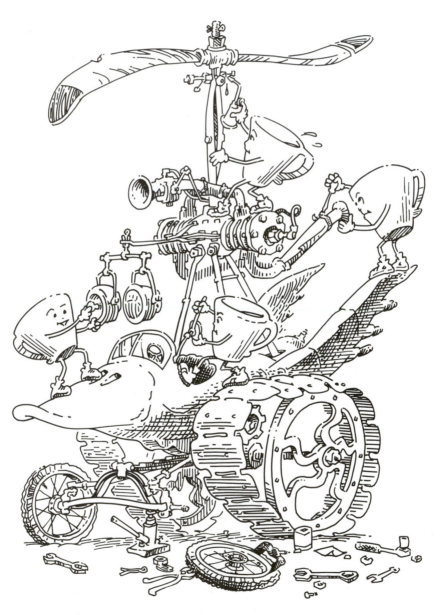

Remember points?

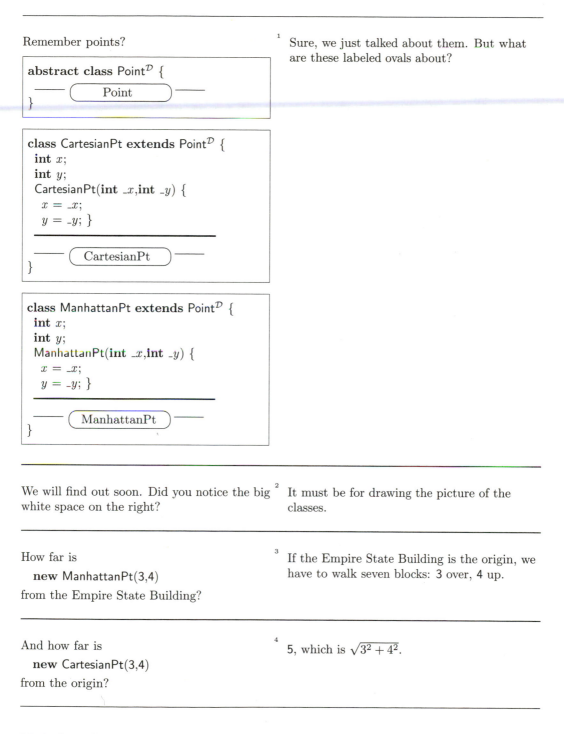

abstract class Point$^{\mathcal{D}}$ {

———(Point)———

}

class CartesianPt extends Point$^{\mathcal{D}}$ {
  int x;
  int y;
  CartesianPt(int $\_x$,int $\_y$) {
   $x = \_x$;
   $y = \_y$; }

———(CartesianPt)———

}

class ManhattanPt extends Point$^{\mathcal{D}}$ {
  int x;
  int y;
  ManhattanPt(int $\_x$,int $\_y$) {
   $x = \_x$;
   $y = \_y$; }

———(ManhattanPt)———

}

[1] Sure, we just talked about them. But what are these labeled ovals about?

We will find out soon. Did you notice the big white space on the right?

[2] It must be for drawing the picture of the classes.

How far is

  new ManhattanPt(3,4)

from the Empire State Building?

[3] If the Empire State Building is the origin, we have to walk seven blocks: 3 over, 4 up.

And how far is

  new CartesianPt(3,4)

from the origin?

[4] 5, which is $\sqrt{3^2 + 4^2}$.

Write the methods $distanceToO$ using {, }, (, ⁵), ;, **return**, **int**, +, $\lfloor\sqrt{\cdot}\rfloor$, and $\cdot^2$, which determine how far a point is from the origin.

Of course, you can't write these methods, yet. Okay, you deserve something sweet for enduring this last question.

What do the methods produce? ⁶

ints, which represent the distances to the origin.

Here they are. ⁷

abstract int $distanceToO$();
Point

int $distanceToO$() {   **return** $\lfloor\sqrt{x^2 + y^2}\rfloor$ ¹; }
CartesianPt

int $distanceToO$() {   **return** $x + y$; }
ManhattanPt

To what do Point, CartesianPt, and ManhattanPt in the boxes refer?

They correspond to the unexplained labels in the definition of the datatype and its variants.

---

¹ When you enter this in a file, use
  (int)Math.sqrt(x*x+y*y).
Math is a class that contains sqrt as a (static) method. Later we will see what (int) means.

The labels remind us that we need to insert ⁸ these methods into Point$^\mathcal{D}$, CartesianPt, and ManhattanPt.

That's simple enough.

How many times have we defined the method ⁹ $distanceToO$?

Three times, but the first one differs from the other two. It is labeled **abstract**, while the others are not preceded by a special word.

Do **abstract** methods belong to the **abstract class**?	10 Yes, they always do.

An **abstract** method in an **abstract** class introduces an obligation, which says that all concrete classes that extend this abstract class[1] must contain a matching method definition.	11 Okay.

[1] Directly or indirectly. That is, the concrete class may extend an abstract class that extends the abstract class with the obligation and so on.

What is the value of
  new ManhattanPt(3,4)
  .$distanceToO()$?
	12 7.

How do we arrive at that value?	13 We determine the value of $x + y,$ with x replaced by 3 and y replaced by 4.

What is the value of
  new CartesianPt(3,4)
  .$distanceToO()$?
	14 5, because that is the value of
	
	    $\sqrt{x^2 + y^2}$
	
	with x replaced by 3 and y replaced by 4.

What does $\lfloor \sqrt{x} \rfloor$ compute?	15 The largest **int** that does not exceed the square root of x.

Time for a short break?	16 An apple a day keeps the dentist away. A cup of coffee does not.

Here is another datatype with its variants. What is different about them?

17 It is like Num$^\mathcal{D}$ but has more variants.

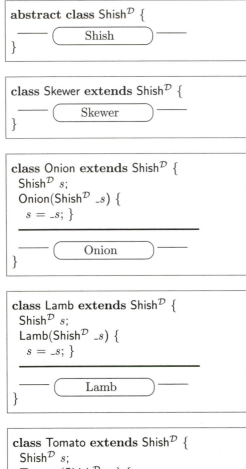

abstract class Shish$^\mathcal{D}$ {
——— (Shish) ———
}

class Skewer **extends** Shish$^\mathcal{D}$ {
——— (Skewer) ———
}

class Onion **extends** Shish$^\mathcal{D}$ {
  Shish$^\mathcal{D}$ s;
  Onion(Shish$^\mathcal{D}$ _s) {
   s = _s; }
———————————
——— (Onion) ———
}

class Lamb **extends** Shish$^\mathcal{D}$ {
  Shish$^\mathcal{D}$ s;
  Lamb(Shish$^\mathcal{D}$ _s) {
   s = _s; }
———————————
——— (Lamb) ———
}

class Tomato **extends** Shish$^\mathcal{D}$ {
  Shish$^\mathcal{D}$ s;
  Tomato(Shish$^\mathcal{D}$ _s) {
   s = _s; }
———————————
——— (Tomato) ———
}

Did you notice the big space on the right?

18 Yes, isn't it for drawing the picture of the classes?

Construct a Shish$^{\mathcal{D}}$.	[19] How about **new** Skewer()?

Yes, every Skewer is also a Shish$^{\mathcal{D}}$. How about another one?	[20] Here's one:
	    new Onion(
	      new Skewer()).

And a third?	[21] Here's one more:
	    new Onion(
	      new Lamb(
	        new Onion(
	          new Skewer())))).

Are there only Onions on this Shish$^{\mathcal{D}}$: **new** Skewer()?	[22] true, because there is neither Lamb nor Tomato on **new** Skewer ().

Are there only Onions on this Shish$^{\mathcal{D}}$:
    new Onion(
      new Skewer())?
	[23] true.

And how about:
    new Lamb(
      new Skewer())?
	[24] false.

Is it true that
    new Onion(
      new Onion(
        new Onion(
          new Skewer()))))
contains only Onions?
	[25] true.

And finally:
    new Onion(
      new Lamb(
        new Onion(
          new Skewer()))))?
	[26] false.

Write the methods *onlyOnions*[1] using {, }, (,), . , ;, true, false, **return**, and **boolean**.

27 Of course, you can't write these methods, yet. Okay, you deserve a lollipop for enduring this kind of question again.

And what do they produce?

28 **boolean**s.

Here are the methods.

> **abstract boolean** *onlyOnions*();
>
> Shish

> **boolean** *onlyOnions*() {
>   **return** true; }
>
> Skewer

> **boolean** *onlyOnions*() {
>   **return** *s.onlyOnions*(); }
>
> Onion

> **boolean** *onlyOnions*() {
>   **return** false; }
>
> Lamb

> **boolean** *onlyOnions*() {
>   **return** false; }
>
> Tomato

Did you notice the labels in the boxes?

29 Yes. We said above that the labeled ovals in the center of the blank lines in the above class definitions tell us where to put the boxes with the corresponding labels.

Good. How many methods have we defined?

30 Five, but the first one is **abstract**; the others are concrete.

Do **abstract** methods belong to the **abstract class**?	[31] Yes, we said so.
Does each variant of Shish$^{\mathcal{D}}$ contain a method called *onlyOnions*?	[32] Yes, because Shish$^{\mathcal{D}}$ contains an **abstract** method called *onlyOnions* that obligates each variant to define a matching, concrete method.
Is this always the case?	[33] Always.
What do these concrete methods consume?	[34] Nothing, just as the **abstract** method says.
What do these concrete methods produce?	[35] **boolean**s, just as the **abstract** method says.

What is the value of
  new Onion(
    new Onion(
      new Skewer()))
  .onlyOnions()?
	[36] true.

And how do we determine the value of
  new Onion(
    new Onion(
      new Skewer()))
  .onlyOnions()?
	[37] We will need to pay attention to the method definitions.

Which definition of *onlyOnions* must we use to determine the value of
  new Onion(
    new Onion(
      new Skewer()))
  .onlyOnions()?
	[38] This object is an instance of Onion, so we need to use the definition of *onlyOnions* that belongs to the Onion variant.

What follows the word **return** in the *onlyOnions* method in Onion?	39 *s.onlyOnions*().

What is the field *s* of the object
  new Onion(
    new Onion(
      new Skewer())))?
	40 It is
	    new Onion(
	      new Skewer()),
	isn't it?

Does *s* always stand for an Onion?	41 No, it has type Shish$^{\mathcal{D}}$, and it can stand for any variant of Shish$^{\mathcal{D}}$: Skewer, Onion, Lamb, or Tomato.

Then what is *s.onlyOnions*()?	42 It should be
	    new Onion(
	      new Skewer())
	    .onlyOnions(),
	right?

Why do we need to know the meaning of
  new Onion(
    new Skewer())
  .onlyOnions()?
	43 Because the answer for
	    new Onion(
	      new Skewer())
	    .onlyOnions()
	is also the answer for
	    new Onion(
	      new Onion(
	        new Skewer()))
	    .onlyOnions().

How do we determine the answer for
  new Onion(
    new Skewer())
  .onlyOnions()?
	44 Let's see.

Which definition of *onlyOnions* must we use to determine the value of **new** Onion(**new** Skewer()) .*onlyOnions*()?	⁴⁵ This object is an instance of **Onion**, so we need to use the definition of *onlyOnions* that belongs to the **Onion** variant.
What follows the word **return** in the *onlyOnions* method in **Onion**?	⁴⁶ *s.onlyOnions*().
What is the field *s* of the object **new** Onion(**new** Skewer())?	⁴⁷ **new** Skewer().

Then what is *s.onlyOnions*()?	⁴⁸ It is
	  new Skewer()
	  .*onlyOnions*(),
	
	just as we would have expected.

Why do we need to know the meaning of
new Skewer()
.*onlyOnions*()?
	⁴⁹ Because the answer for
	  new Skewer()
	  .*onlyOnions*()
	is also the answer for
	  new Onion(
	    new Skewer())
	  .*onlyOnions*(),
	which in turn is the answer for
	  new Onion(
	    new Onion(
	      new Skewer()))
	  .*onlyOnions*().

How do we determine the answer for **new** Skewer() .*onlyOnions*()?	⁵⁰ We need to determine one more time which version of *onlyOnions* we must use.

Is

  new Skewer()

a

  Skewer?

51   Obviously.

Then what is the answer?

52   true.

Why?

53   Because true is what the *onlyOnions* method in Skewer always **return**s.

Are we done?

54   Yes! The answer for
    new Onion(
     new Onion(
      new Skewer()))
    .*onlyOnions*()

is the same as the answer for
    new Onion(
     new Skewer())
    .*onlyOnions*(),

which is the same as the answer for
    new Skewer()
    .*onlyOnions*(),

which is

    true.

What is the value of
  new Onion(
   new Lamb(
    new Skewer()))
  .*onlyOnions*()?

55   false, isn't it?

Which definition of *onlyOnions* must we use to determine the value of
  new Onion(
   new Lamb(
    new Skewer()))
  .*onlyOnions*()?

56   This object is an instance of Onion, so we need to use the definition of *onlyOnions* that belongs to the Onion variant.

What follows the word **return** in the *onlyOnions* method in Onion?	[57] *s.onlyOnions*().

What is the field *s* of the object
  new Onion(
    new Lamb(
      new Skewer())))?
	[58] It is the object built from
	  new Lamb(
	    new Skewer()).

Then what is *s.onlyOnions*()?	[59] It is
	  new Lamb(
	    new Skewer())
	  .onlyOnions(),
	of course.

Why do we need to know the meaning of
  new Lamb(
    new Skewer())
  .onlyOnions()?
	[60] Because the answer for
	  new Lamb(
	    new Skewer())
	  .onlyOnions()
	
	is also the answer for
	  new Onion(
	    new Lamb(
	      new Skewer()))
	  .onlyOnions().

How do we determine the answer for
  new Lamb(
    new Skewer())
  .onlyOnions()?
	[61] We determine which version of *onlyOnions* to use.

And?	[62] We use the one that belongs to Lamb.

And now what is the answer?	[63] false, because false follows the word **return** in the corresponding method definition in Lamb.

Are we done?	[64] Yes! The answer for
	new Onion(
	  new Lamb(
	    new Skewer()))
	.onlyOnions()
	
	is the same as the answer for
	new Lamb(
	  new Skewer())
	.onlyOnions(),
	
	which is
	
	false.

Describe the methods (*i.e.*, the function) *onlyOnions* in your own words.	[65] Here are our words: "The methods determine for a Shish$^{\mathcal{D}}$ whether its contents are edible by an onion lover."

Describe how the methods (*i.e.*, the function) *onlyOnions* accomplish this.	[66] Here are our words again: "For each layer of the Shish$^{\mathcal{D}}$, except for Onion, the corresponding method knows whether it is good or bad. The method for Onion needs to determine whether the remaining layers are only Onions sitting on a Skewer."

Is
  new Tomato(
    new Skewer())
a Shish$^{\mathcal{D}}$?
	[67] Yes.

Is
  new Onion(
    new Tomato(
      new Skewer()))
a Shish$^{\mathcal{D}}$?
	[68] The object
	  new Tomato(
	    new Skewer())
	is an instance of Shish$^{\mathcal{D}}$, so we can also wrap an Onion around it.

And how about another Tomato?	[69] Sure.

Is

    new Tomato(
      new Onion(
        new Tomato(
          new Skewer())))

a vegetarian shish kebab?

And
    new Onion(
      new Onion(
        new Onion(
          new Skewer()))))?

Define the methods (*i.e.*, the function)

    isVegetarian,

which return **true** if the given object does not contain **Lamb**.
Hint: The method for tomatoes is the same as the one for onions.

---

[70] Of course, there is no **Lamb** on it.

---

[71] Yes, it is a vegetarian shish kebab, because it only contains Onions.

---

[72] That's no big deal now.

---

abstract boolean *isVegetarian*();

Shish

---

boolean *isVegetarian*() {
  return true; }

Skewer

---

boolean *isVegetarian*() {
  return *s.isVegetarian*(); }

Onion

---

boolean *isVegetarian*() {
  return false; }

Lamb

---

boolean *isVegetarian*() {
  return *s.isVegetarian*(); }

Tomato

How many methods have we defined?	[73] Five: one **abstract**, the others concrete.
Do **abstract** methods belong to the **abstract class**?	[74] Yes, they always do.
Does each variant of $\mathsf{Shish}^{\mathcal{D}}$ contain a method called *isVegetarian*?	[75] Yes, because $\mathsf{Shish}^{\mathcal{D}}$ contains an **abstract** method called *isVegetarian*.
Is this always the case?	[76] Always.
What do these concrete methods consume?	[77] Nothing, just as the **abstract** method says.
What do these concrete methods produce?	[78] **boolean**s, just as the **abstract** method says.

The Second Bit of Advice

*When writing a function over a
datatype, place a method in each of the
variants that make up the datatype. If
a field of a variant belongs to the same
datatype, the method may call the
corresponding method of the field in
computing the function.*

Collect all the pieces of Shish$^\mathcal{D}$. Here is the datatype.

```
abstract class Shish^D {
  abstract boolean onlyOnions();
  abstract boolean isVegetarian();
}
```

There are two methods per variant.

```
class Skewer extends Shish^D {
  boolean onlyOnions() {
    return true; }
  boolean isVegetarian() {
    return true; }
}
```

```
class Onion extends Shish^D {
  Shish^D s;
  Onion(Shish^D _s) {
    s = _s; }

  boolean onlyOnions() {
    return s.onlyOnions(); }
  boolean isVegetarian() {
    return s.isVegetarian(); }
}
```

```
class Lamb extends Shish^D {
  Shish^D s;
  Lamb(Shish^D _s) {
    s = _s; }

  boolean onlyOnions() {
    return false; }
  boolean isVegetarian() {
    return false; }
}
```

```
class Tomato extends Shish^D {
  Shish^D s;
  Tomato(Shish^D _s) {
    s = _s; }

  boolean onlyOnions() {
    return false; }
  boolean isVegetarian() {
    return s.isVegetarian(); }
}
```

What do the following define?

80 They define a datatype and four variants that are similar in shape to $Shish^{\mathcal{D}}$.

```
abstract class Kebab^D {
——— ( Kebab ) ———
}
```

```
class Holder extends Kebab^D {
  Object o;
  Holder(Object _o) {
    o = _o; }

——————————————————
——— ( Holder ) ———
}
```

```
class Shallot extends Kebab^D {
  Kebab^D k;
  Shallot(Kebab^D _k) {
    k = _k; }

——————————————————
——— ( Shallot ) ———
}
```

```
class Shrimp extends Kebab^D {
  Kebab^D k;
  Shrimp(Kebab^D _k) {
    k = _k; }

——————————————————
——— ( Shrimp ) ———
}
```

```
class Radish extends Kebab^D {
  Kebab^D k;
  Radish(Kebab^D _k) {
    k = _k; }

——————————————————
——— ( Radish ) ———
}
```

Don't forget the picture.

What is different about them?

81

They are placed onto different **Holders**.

Here are some holders.

```
abstract class Rod^D {}
```

```
class Dagger extends Rod^D {}
```

```
class Sabre extends Rod^D {}
```

```
class Sword extends Rod^D {}
```

Are they good ones?

82

Sure, a rod is a kind of holder, and every rod is an **Object**, so *o* in **Holder** can stand for any rod. Is it necessary to draw another picture?

Think of another kind of holder. Are you tired of drawing pictures, yet?

83

We could move all of the food to various forms of plates.

```
abstract class Plate^D {}
```

```
class Gold extends Plate^D {}
```

```
class Silver extends Plate^D {}
```

```
class Brass extends Plate^D {}
```

```
class Copper extends Plate^D {}
```

```
class Wood extends Plate^D {}
```

What is
```
new Shallot(
  new Radish(
    new Holder(
      new Dagger()))))?
```

84

It's a Kebab^D.

Is
  new Shallot(
   new Radish(
    new Holder(
     new Dagger()))))
a vegetarian Kebab$^{\mathcal{D}}$?

85

Sure it is. It only contains radishes and shallots.

Is
  new Shallot(
   new Radish(
    new Holder(
     new Gold()))))
a Kebab$^{\mathcal{D}}$?

86

Sure, because Gold is a Plate$^{\mathcal{D}}$, Plate$^{\mathcal{D}}$ is used as a Holder, and radishes and shallots can be put on any Holder.

Is
  new Shallot(
   new Radish(
    new Holder(
     new Gold()))))
a vegetarian kebab?

87

Sure it is. It is basically like
  new Shallot(
   new Radish(
    new Holder(
     new Dagger())))),

except that we have moved all the food from a Dagger to a Gold plate.

Let's define the methods (*i.e.*, the function)
  isVeggie,
which check whether a kebab contains only vegetarian foods, regardless of what Holder it is on.

88

If you can, you may rest now.

Write the abstract method *isVeggie*.

89

That's possible now.

abstract boolean *isVeggie*()
Kebab

Of course, *isVeggie* belongs to Kebab$^{\mathcal{D}}$ and *isVegetarian* to Shish$^{\mathcal{D}}$.

The concrete methods are similar to those called *isVegetarian*. Here are two more; define the remaining two.

```
boolean isVeggie() {
  return true; }
```
Holder

```
boolean isVeggie() {
  return k.isVeggie(); }
```
Shallot

90 Except for the names of the methods and fields, the definitions are the same as they were for Shish$^{\mathcal{D}}$.

```
boolean isVeggie() {
  return false; }
```
Shrimp

```
boolean isVeggie() {
  return k.isVeggie(); }
```
Radish

What is the value of
  new Shallot(
    new Radish(
      new Holder(
        new Dagger()))))
.*isVeggie*()?

91 true.

What is
  new Shallot(
    new Radish(
      new Holder(
        new Dagger()))))?

92 It is a Kebab$^{\mathcal{D}}$, but we also know that it is an instance of the Shallot variant.

What is the value of
  new Shallot(
    new Radish(
      new Holder(
        new Gold()))))
.*isVeggie*()?

93 It is true, too.

And what is
  new Shallot(
    new Radish(
      new Holder(
        new Gold()))))?

94 It is also a Kebab$^{\mathcal{D}}$, because any kind of Holder will do.

Methods to Our Madness

What type of value is
  new Shallot(
  new Radish(
   new Holder(
    new Integer(52))))
 .*isVeggie*()?

⁹⁵ **boolean.**

What type of value is
  new Shallot(
  new Radish(
   new Holder(
    new OneMoreThan(
     new Zero())))))
 .*isVeggie*()?

⁹⁶ **boolean.**

What type of value is
  new Shallot(
  new Radish(
   new Holder(
    new Boolean(false))))
 .*isVeggie*()?

⁹⁷ **boolean.**

Does that mean *isVeggie* works for all five kinds of **Holder**s?

⁹⁸ Yes, and all other kinds of **Object**s that we could possibly think of.

What is the holder of
  new Shallot(
  new Radish(
   new Holder(
    new Dagger()))))?

⁹⁹ All the food is on a **Dagger**.

What is the holder of
  new Shallot(
  new Radish(
   new Holder(
    new Gold()))))?

¹⁰⁰ All the food is now on a **Gold** plate.

What is the holder of
  new Shallot(
    new Radish(
      new Holder(
        new Integer(52))))?

101   All the food is on an Integer.

What is the value of
  new Shallot(
    new Radish(
      new Holder(
        new Dagger()))))
.*whatHolder*()?

102   The dagger.

What is the value of
  new Shallot(
    new Radish(
      new Holder(
        new Gold()))))
.*whatHolder*()?

103   The gold plate.

What is the value of
  new Shallot(
    new Radish(
      new Holder(
        new Integer(52))))
.*whatHolder*()?

104   An Integer, whose underlying **int** is 52.

What type of values do the methods (*i.e.,* the function) of *whatHolder* produce?

105   They produce rods, plates, and integers. And it looks like they can produce a lot more.

Is there a simple way of saying what type of values they produce?

106   They always produce an Object, which is also the type of the field of Holder.

Here is the abstract method *whatHolder*.

abstract Object *whatHolder*()
Kebab

107   If we add this method to Kebab$^{\mathcal{D}}$, then we must add a method definition to each of the four variants.

What is the value of
  new Holder(
   new Integer(52))
  .*whatHolder*()?

108 **new** Integer(52).

What is the value of
  new Holder(
   new Sword())
  .*whatHolder*()?

109 **new** Sword().

What is the value of
  new Holder(*b*)
  .*whatHolder*()
if *b* is some object?

110 It is *b*.

Define the concrete method that goes into
the space labeled Holder.

111 With these kinds of hints, it's easy.

> Object *whatHolder*() {
> **return** *o*; }
>
>   Holder

What is the value of
  new Radish(
   new Shallot(
    new Shrimp(
     new Holder(
      new Integer(52)))))
  .*whatHolder*()?

112 **new** Integer(52).

What is the value of
  new Shallot(
   new Shrimp(
    new Holder(
     new Integer(52))))
  .*whatHolder*()?

113 **new** Integer(52).

What is the value of
  new Shrimp(
    new Holder(
     new Integer(52)))
  .*whatHolder*()?

114

new Integer(52).

Does that mean that the value of
  new Radish(
    new Shallot(
    new Shrimp(
     new Holder(
      new Integer(52)))))
  .*whatHolder*()
is the same as
  new Shallot(
    new Shrimp(
    new Holder(
     new Integer(52))))
  .*whatHolder*(),
which is the same as
  new Shrimp(
    new Holder(
    new Integer(52)))
  .*whatHolder*(),
which is the same as
  new Holder(
    new Integer(52))
  .*whatHolder*()?

115

Yes, all four have the same answer:
  new Integer(52).

Here is the method for Shallot.

```
Object whatHolder() {
  return k.whatHolder(); }
```
                          Shallot

Write the methods of *whatHolder* for Shrimp and Radish.

116

They are all the same.

```
Object whatHolder() {
  return k.whatHolder(); }
```
                          Shrimp

```
Object whatHolder() {
  return k.whatHolder(); }
```
                          Radish

Here is the datatype and one of its variants. There are only three left.

```
abstract class KebabᴰᐟD {
  abstract boolean isVeggie();
  abstract Object whatHolder();
}
```

```
class Holder extends Kebabᴰ {
  Object o;
  Holder(Object _o) {
    o = _o; }

  boolean isVeggie() {
    return true; }
  Object whatHolder() {
    return o; }
}
```

Collect the remaining variants.

```
class Shallot extends Kebabᴰ {
  Kebabᴰ k;
  Shallot(Kebabᴰ _k) {
    k = _k; }

  boolean isVeggie() {
    return k.isVeggie(); }
  Object whatHolder() {
    return k.whatHolder(); }
}
```

```
class Shrimp extends Kebabᴰ {
  Kebabᴰ k;
  Shrimp(Kebabᴰ _k) {
    k = _k; }

  boolean isVeggie() {
    return false; }
  Object whatHolder() {
    return k.whatHolder(); }
}
```

```
class Radish extends Kebabᴰ {
  Kebabᴰ k;
  Radish(Kebabᴰ _k) {
    k = _k; }

  boolean isVeggie() {
    return k.isVeggie(); }
  Object whatHolder() {
    return k.whatHolder(); }
}
```

Are there any other Kebabᴰ foods besides Shallot, Shrimp, and Radish? No, these are the only kinds of foods on a Kebabᴰ.

Can we add more foods?

¹¹⁹ Sure. We did something like that when we added Thyme and Sage to Seasoning$^\mathcal{D}$.

Let's define another Kebab$^\mathcal{D}$.

```
class Pepper extends Kebab^D {
  Kebab^D k;
  Pepper(Kebab^D _k) {
    k = _k; }

  boolean isVeggie() {
    return k.isVeggie(); }
  Object whatHolder() {
    return k.whatHolder(); }
}
```

Why does it include *isVeggie* and *whatHolder* methods?

¹²⁰ A concrete class that extends Kebab$^\mathcal{D}$ must define these two methods. That's what the **abstract** specifications say. We can define as many Kebab$^\mathcal{D}$s as we wish.

```
class Zucchini extends Kebab^D {
  Kebab^D k;
  Zucchini(Kebab^D _k) {
    k = _k; }

  boolean isVeggie() {
    return k.isVeggie(); }
  Object whatHolder() {
    return k.whatHolder(); }
}
```

Is it obvious how the new methods work?

¹²¹ Totally. In both cases *isVeggie* just checks the rest of the Kebab$^\mathcal{D}$, because green peppers and zucchini are vegetables. Similarly, *whatHolder* returns whatever holder belongs to the rest of the Kebab$^\mathcal{D}$.

And then there were six.

¹²² Yes, now Kebab$^\mathcal{D}$ has six variants.

Which of these points is closer to the origin:

new ManhattanPt(3,4)

and

new ManhattanPt(1,5)?

¹²³ The second one,
because its distance to the origin is 6 while the first point's distance is 7.

Good. Which of the following points is closer to the origin:

new CartesianPt(3,4)

or

new CartesianPt(12,5)?

¹²⁴ The first one, clearly. Its distance to the origin is 5, but the second distance is 13.

We added the method *closerToO* to CartesianPt. It consumes another CartesianPt and determines whether the constructed or the consumed point is closer to the origin.

The definitions are nearly identical. The method for ManhattanPt consumes a ManhattanPt and determines which of those two points is closer to the origin.

```
class CartesianPt extends Pointᴰ {
  int x;
  int y;
  CartesianPt(int _x,int _y) {
    x = _x;
    y = _y; }
```
___
```
  int distanceToO() {
    return ⌊√(x² + y²)⌋; }
  boolean closerToO(CartesianPt p) {
    return
      distanceToO() ≤ p.distanceToO(); }
}
```

```
class ManhattanPt extends Pointᴰ {
  int x;
  int y;
  ManhattanPt(int _x,int _y) {
    x = _x;
    y = _y; }
```
___
```
  int distanceToO() {
    return x + y; }
  boolean closerToO(ManhattanPt p) {
    return
      distanceToO() ≤¹ p.distanceToO(); }
}
```

Add the corresponding method to ManhattanPt.

___

[1] This is the two character symbol <=.

What is the value of
 new ManhattanPt(3,4)
 .*closerToO*(**new** ManhattanPt(1,5))?

false.

What is the value of
 new ManhattanPt(1,5)
 .*closerToO*(**new** ManhattanPt(3,4))?

true, obviously.

What is the value of
 new CartesianPt(12,5)
 .*closerToO*(**new** CartesianPt(3,4))?

false, and true is the value of
 new CartesianPt(3,4)
 .*closerToO*(**new** CartesianPt(12,5)).

So finally, what is the value of
 new CartesianPt(3,4)
 .*closerToO*(**new** ManhattanPt(1,5))?

That's nonsense.

Why?	**130** The method *closerToO* can only consume CartesianPts, not ManhattanPts.

How can we fix that?	**131** We could replace (CartesianPt p) by (Point$^{\mathcal{D}}$ p) in the definition of *closerToO* for CartesianPt.

If we do that, can we still determine the value of $p.distanceToO()$?	**132** Yes, because the definition of Point$^{\mathcal{D}}$ obligates every variant to provide a method named *distanceToO*.

Why does it help to replace (CartesianPt p) by (Point$^{\mathcal{D}}$ p)?	**133** Every CartesianPt is a Point$^{\mathcal{D}}$, and every ManhattanPt is a Point$^{\mathcal{D}}$, too.

Here is the improved CartesianPt.

134 Easy.

```
class CartesianPt extends PointD {
  int x;
  int y;
  CartesianPt(int _x,int _y) {
    x = _x;
    y = _y; }

  int distanceToO() {
    return ⌊√(x² + y²)⌋; }
  boolean closerToO(PointD p) {
    return
      distanceToO() ≤ p.distanceToO(); }
}
```

```
class ManhattanPt extends PointD {
  int x;
  int y;
  ManhattanPt(int _x,int _y) {
    x = _x;
    y = _y; }

  int distanceToO() {
    return x + y; }
  boolean closerToO(PointD p) {
    return
      distanceToO() ≤ p.distanceToO(); }
}
```

Improve the definition of ManhattanPt.

Is the definition of *closerToO* in CartesianPt the same as the one in ManhattanPt?	**135** Yes, they are identical.

Correct, and therefore we can add a copy to the abstract class Point$^{\mathcal{D}}$ and delete the definitions from the variants.

```
abstract class PointD {
  boolean closerToO1(PointD p) {
    return
      distanceToO() ≤ p.distanceToO(); }
  abstract int distanceToO();
}
```

136 Looks correct.

[1] The method closerToO is a *template* and the method distanceToO is a *hook* in the *template method* pattern instance [4].

What else do the two point variants have in common?

137 Their fields. Shouldn't we lift them, too?

Yes. It's tricky, but here is a start.

```
abstract class PointD {
  int x;
  int y;
  PointD(int _x,int _y) {
    x = _x;
    y = _y; }

  boolean closerToO(PointD p) {
    return
      distanceToO() ≤ p.distanceToO(); }
  abstract int distanceToO();
}
```

138 This not only lifts x and y, it also introduces a new constructor.

Absolutely. And we need to change how a CartesianPt is built. Define ManhattanPt.

```
class CartesianPt extends PointD {
  CartesianPt(int _x,int _y) {
    super(_x,_y); }

  int distanceToO() {
    return ⌊√(x² + y²)⌋; }
}
```

139 Mimicking this change is easy. But what does **super**(_x,_y) mean?

```
class ManhattanPt extends PointD {
  ManhattanPt(int _x,int _y) {
    super(_x,_y); }

  int distanceToO() {
    return x + y; }
}
```

The expressions **super**$(\_x,\_y)$ in the constructors CartesianPt and ManhattanPt create a Point$^{\mathcal{D}}$ with the appropriate fields, and the respective constructor guarantees that the point becomes a CartesianPt or a ManhattanPt.

140 That's simple.

Do we now have everything that characterizes Point$^{\mathcal{D}}$s in the datatype?

141 Yes, and those things that distinguish the two variants from each other reside in the corresponding variants.

Is this a long chapter?

142 Yes, let's have a short snack break.

3.
What's New?

Do you like to eat pizza?

```
abstract class Pizza^D {
____ ( Pizza )  ____
}
```

```
class Crust extends Pizza^D {
____ ( Crust )  ____
}
```

```
class Cheese extends Pizza^D {
  Pizza^D p;
  Cheese(Pizza^D _p) {
   p = _p; }
  _____
____ ( Cheese )  ____
}
```

```
class Olive extends Pizza^D {
  Pizza^D p;
  Olive(Pizza^D _p) {
   p = _p; }
  _____
____ ( Olive )  ____
}
```

```
class Anchovy extends Pizza^D {
  Pizza^D p;
  Anchovy(Pizza^D _p) {
   p = _p; }
  _____
____ ( Anchovy )  ____
}
```

[1] Looks like good toppings. Let's add **Sausage**.

```
class Sausage extends Pizza^D {
  Pizza^D p;
  Sausage(Pizza^D _p) {
   p = _p; }
  _____
____ ( Sausage )  ____
}
```

Here is our favorite pizza:
    new Anchovy(
      new Olive(
        new Anchovy(
          new Anchovy(
            new Cheese(
              new Crust())))))).

2   This looks too salty.

How about removing the anchovies?

3   That would make it less salty.

Let's remove them. What is the value of
    new Anchovy(
      new Olive(
        new Anchovy(
          new Anchovy(
            new Cheese(
              new Crust()))))))
    .remA[1]()?

4   It should be a cheese and olive pizza, like
    this:
        new Olive(
          new Cheese(
            new Crust())).

---

[1] A better name for these methods would be `removeAnchovy`,
but then our definitions wouldn't fit into these columns.

What is the value of
    new Sausage(
      new Olive(
        new Anchovy(
          new Sausage(
            new Cheese(
              new Crust()))))))
    .remA()?

5   It should be a cheese, sausage, and olive
    pizza, like this:
        new Sausage(
          new Olive(
            new Sausage(
              new Cheese(
                new Crust()))))).

Does *remA* belong to the datatype $\mathsf{Pizza}^{\mathcal{D}}$
and its variants?

6   Yes, and it produces them, too.

Chapter 3

Define the methods that belong to the five variants. Here is a start.

abstract Pizza$^\mathcal{D}$ *remA*();
Pizza

Pizza$^\mathcal{D}$ *remA*() {   **return new** Crust(); }
Crust

7 We didn't expect you to know this one.

Define the two methods that belong to Olive and Sausage. We've eaten the cheese already.

Pizza$^\mathcal{D}$ *remA*() {   **return new** Cheese($p.remA$()); }
Cheese

8 The Olive and Sausage methods are similar to the Cheese method.

Pizza$^\mathcal{D}$ *remA*() {   **return new** Olive($p.remA$()); }
Olive

Pizza$^\mathcal{D}$ *remA*() {   **return new** Sausage($p.remA$()); }
Sausage

Explain why we use
  new Cheese ... ,
  new Olive ... , and
  new Sausage ...
when we define these methods.

9 The cheese, the olives, and the sausages on the pizzas must be put back on top of the pizza that $p.remA$() produces.

The methods *remA* must produce a Pizza$^\mathcal{D}$, so let's use **new** Crust(), the simplest Pizza$^\mathcal{D}$, for the method in Anchovy.

Pizza$^\mathcal{D}$ *remA*() {   **return new** Crust(); }
Anchovy

10 Yes, and now the methods of *remA* produce pizzas without any anchovies on them.

Let's try it out on a small pizza:
    new Anchovy(
      new Crust())
    .remA().

11 That's easy. The object is an Anchovy. So the answer is **new** Crust().

Is
    new Crust()
like
    new Anchovy(
      new Crust())
without anchovy?

12 Absolutely, but what if we had more anchovies?

No problem. Here is an example:
    new Anchovy(
      new Anchovy(
        new Crust()))
    .remA().

13 That's easy again. As before, the object is an Anchovy so that the answer must still be **new** Crust().

Okay, so what if we had an olive and cheese on top:
    new Olive(
     new Cheese(
      new Anchovy(
       new Anchovy(
        new Crust()))))
    .remA()?

14 Well, this object is an Olive and its p stands for
    new Cheese(
     new Anchovy(
      new Anchovy(
       new Crust())))).

Then, what is the value of
    new Olive($p.remA$())
where p stands for
    new Cheese(
     new Anchovy(
      new Anchovy(
       new Crust()))))?

15 It is the pizza that
    new Cheese(
     new Anchovy(
      new Anchovy(
       new Crust())))
    .remA()
produces, with an olive added on top.

What is the value of
  new Cheese(
    new Anchovy(
      new Anchovy(
        new Crust()))).
.*remA*()?

¹⁶ It is
  new Cheese($p.remA()$),
where p stands for
  new Anchovy(
    new Anchovy(
      new Crust())).

And what is the value of
  new Cheese(
    new Anchovy(
      new Anchovy(
        new Crust()))
    .*remA*())?

¹⁷ It is the pizza that
  new Anchovy(
    new Anchovy(
      new Crust()))
  .*remA*()
produces, with cheese added on top.

Do we know the value of
  new Anchovy(
    new Anchovy(
      new Crust()))
  .*remA*()?

¹⁸ Yes, we know that it produces **new** Crust().

Does that mean that **new** Crust() is the answer?

¹⁹ No, we still have to add cheese and an olive.

Does it matter in which order we add those two toppings?

²⁰ Yes, we must first add cheese, producing
  new Cheese(
    new Crust())
and then we add the olive.

So what is the final answer?

²¹ It is
  new Olive(
    new Cheese(
      new Crust())).

Let's try one more example:
    new Cheese(
      new Anchovy(
        new Cheese(
          new Crust()))))
    .remA().
What kind of pizza should this make?

22 It should be a double-cheese pizza.

Check it out!

23 The object is an instance of **Cheese** so the
value is
$$\text{new Cheese}(p.remA())$$
where p stands for
    new Anchovy(
      new Cheese(
        new Crust())).

Doesn't that mean that the result is
    new Cheese(
      new Anchovy(
        new Cheese(
          new Crust()))
      .remA())?

24 Yes, it puts the cheese on whatever we get
for
    new Anchovy(
      new Cheese(
        new Crust()))
    .remA().

What about
    new Anchovy(
      new Cheese(
        new Crust()))
    .remA()?

25 Now the object is an anchovy.

And the answer is
    new Crust()?

26 Yes, but we need to add cheese on top.

Does that mean the final answer is
    new Cheese(
      new Crust())?

27 Yes, though it's not the answer we want.

What do we want?	²⁸ A double-cheese pizza like
	    new Cheese(
	      new Cheese(
	        new Crust())),
	
	because that's what it means to remove anchovies and nothing else.

Which *remA* method do we need to change to get the cheese back?	²⁹ The one in Anchovy.

$Pizza^\mathcal{D}$ *remA*() {
  return *p.remA*(); }

Anchovy

Does this *remA* still belong to $Pizza^\mathcal{D}$?	³⁰ Yes, and it still produces them.

The Third Bit of Advice

*When writing a function that returns values of a datatype, use **new** to create these values.*

We could add cheese on top of the anchovies.	³¹ Yes, that would hide their taste, too.

What kind of pizza is
  new Olive(
   new Anchovy(
   new Cheese(
   new Anchovy(
   new Crust())))))
.*topAwC*¹()?
	³² Easy, it adds cheese on top of each anchovy:
	  new Olive(
	   new <u>Cheese</u>(
	   new Anchovy(
	   new Cheese(
	   new <u>Cheese</u>(
	   new Anchovy(
	   new Crust()))))))).

---

¹ A better name for these methods would be `topAnchovywithCheese`.

Did you notice the underlines?	³³ Yes, they show where we added cheese.

And what is
  new Olive(
    new Cheese(
      new Sausage(
        new Crust()))))
  .$topAwC()$?

Here we don't add any cheese, because the pizza does not contain any anchovies:
  new Olive(
    new Cheese(
      new Sausage(
        new Crust()))).

Define the remaining methods.

> **abstract** Pizza$^\mathcal{D}$ $topAwC()$;
>
> Pizza

> Pizza$^\mathcal{D}$ $topAwC()$ {
>   **return new** Crust(); }
>
> Crust

We expect you to know some of the answers.

> Pizza$^\mathcal{D}$ $topAwC()$ {
>   **return new** Cheese($p.topAwC()$); }
>
> Cheese

> Pizza$^\mathcal{D}$ $topAwC()$ {
>   **return new** Olive($p.topAwC()$); }
>
> Olive

> Pizza$^\mathcal{D}$ $topAwC()$ {
>   **return new** Sausage($p.topAwC()$); }
>
> Sausage

Take a look at this method.

> Pizza$^\mathcal{D}$ $topAwC()$ {
>   **return** $p.topAwC()$; }
>
> Anchovy

With that definition, $topAwC$ would give the same results as $remA$. The method $topAwC$ in Anchovy must put the anchovy back on the pizza and top it with cheese.

> Pizza$^\mathcal{D}$ $topAwC()$ {
>   **return**
>   **new** Cheese(
>   **new** Anchovy($p.topAwC()$)); }
>
> Anchovy

How many layers of cheese are in the result of

  (**new** Olive(
    new Anchovy(
      new Cheese(
        new Anchovy(
          new Crust()))))
  .$remA$())
  .$topAwC$()?

37   One, because $remA$ removes all the anchovies, so that $topAwC$ doesn't add any cheese.

How many occurrences of cheese are in the result of

  (**new** Olive(
    new Anchovy(
      new Cheese(
        new Anchovy(
          new Crust()))))
  .$topAwC$())
  .$remA$()?

38   Three, because $topAwC$ first adds cheese for each anchovy. Then $remA$ removes all the anchovies:

    new Olive(
      new Cheese(
        new Cheese(
          new Cheese(
            new Crust()))))).

Perhaps we should replace every anchovy with cheese.

39   We just did something like that.

Is it true that for each anchovy in x

  $x.topAwC().remA()$

adds some cheese?

40   Yes, and it does more. Once all the cheese is added, the anchovies are removed.

So

  $x.topAwC().remA()$

is a way to substitute all anchovies with cheese by looking at each topping of a pizza and adding cheese on top of each anchovy and then looking at each topping again, including all the new cheese, and removing the anchovies.

41   Aha!

Here is a different description:

"The methods look at each topping of a pizza and replace each anchovy with cheese."

Define the methods that match this description. Call them $subAbC$.[1] Here is the abstract method.

abstract Pizza$^{\mathcal{D}}$ $subAbC$();
Pizza

---

[1] A better name for these methods would be `substituteAnchovybyCheese`.

---

42 Here is a skeleton.

Pizza$^{\mathcal{D}}$ $subAbC$() {   **return new** Crust(); }
Crust

Pizza$^{\mathcal{D}}$ $subAbC$() {   **return new** Cheese($p.subAbC$()); }
Cheese

Pizza$^{\mathcal{D}}$ $subAbC$() {   **return new** Olive($p.subAbC$()); }
Olive

Pizza$^{\mathcal{D}}$ $subAbC$() {   **return** _____ ; }
Anchovy

Pizza$^{\mathcal{D}}$ $subAbC$() {   **return new** Sausage($p.subAbC$()); }
Sausage

Does this skeleton look familiar?

43 Yes, this skeleton looks just like those of $topAwC$ and $remA$.

Define the method that belongs in Anchovy.

44 Here it is.

Pizza$^{\mathcal{D}}$ $subAbC$() {   **return new** Cheese($p.subAbC$()); }
Anchovy

Collection time.[1]

The classes are getting larger.

```
abstract class Pizza^D {
  abstract Pizza^D remA();
  abstract Pizza^D topAwC();
  abstract Pizza^D subAbC();
}
```

```
class Crust extends Pizza^D {
  Pizza^D remA() {
    return new Crust(); }
  Pizza^D topAwC() {
    return new Crust(); }
  Pizza^D subAbC() {
    return new Crust(); }
}
```

```
class Cheese extends Pizza^D {
  Pizza^D p;
  Cheese(Pizza^D _p) {
    p = _p; }

  Pizza^D remA() {
    return new Cheese(p.remA()); }
  Pizza^D topAwC() {
    return new Cheese(p.topAwC()); }
  Pizza^D subAbC() {
    return new Cheese(p.subAbC()); }
}
```

```
class Olive extends Pizza^D {
  Pizza^D p;
  Olive(Pizza^D _p) {
    p = _p; }

  Pizza^D remA() {
    return new Olive(p.remA()); }
  Pizza^D topAwC() {
    return new Olive(p.topAwC()); }
  Pizza^D subAbC() {
    return new Olive(p.subAbC()); }
}
```

```
class Anchovy extends Pizza^D {
  Pizza^D p;
  Anchovy(Pizza^D _p) {
    p = _p; }

  Pizza^D remA() {
    return p.remA(); }
  Pizza^D topAwC() {
    return
      new Cheese(
        new Anchovy(p.topAwC())); }
  Pizza^D subAbC() {
    return new Cheese(p.subAbC()); }
}
```

```
class Sausage extends Pizza^D {
  Pizza^D p;
  Sausage(Pizza^D _p) {
    p = _p; }

  Pizza^D remA() {
    return new Sausage(p.remA()); }
  Pizza^D topAwC() {
    return new Sausage(p.topAwC()); }
  Pizza^D subAbC() {
    return new Sausage(p.subAbC()); }
}
```

---

[1] This is similar to the *interpreter* and *composite* patterns [4].

Let's add more Pizza$^{\mathcal{D}}$ foods.

⁴⁶ Good idea.

Here is one addition: Spinach.

```
class Spinach extends Pizza𝒟 {
  Pizza𝒟 p;
  Spinach(Pizza𝒟 _p) {
    p = _p; }

  Pizza𝒟 remA() {
    return new Spinach(p.remA()); }
  Pizza𝒟 topAwC() {
    return new Spinach(p.topAwC()); }
  Pizza𝒟 subAbC() {
    return new Spinach(p.subAbC()); }
}
```

⁴⁷ Yes, we must define three concrete methods for each variant of Pizza$^{\mathcal{D}}$.

Do we need to change Pizza$^{\mathcal{D}}$, Crust, Cheese, Olive, Anchovy, or Sausage?

⁴⁸ No. When we add variants to the datatypes we have defined, we don't need to change what we have.

Isn't that neat?

⁴⁹ Yes, this is a really flexible way of defining classes and methods. Unfortunately, the more things we want to do with Pizza$^{\mathcal{D}}$s, the more methods we must add.

True enough. And that means cluttered classes. Is there a better way to express all this?

⁵⁰ That would be great, because these definitions are painful to the eye. But we don't know of a better way to organize these definitions yet.

Don't worry. We are about to discover how to make more sense out of such things.

⁵¹ Great.

And now you can replace anchovy with whatever pizza topping you want.

⁵² We will stick with anchovies.

4.
Come to Our Carousel

Wasn't this last collection overwhelming?	[1] It sure was. We defined seven classes and each contained three method definitions.
Could it get worse?	[2] It sure could. For everything we want to do with Pizza$^\mathcal{D}$, we must add a method definition to each class.
Why does that become overwhelming?	[3] Because it becomes more and more difficult to understand the rationale for each of the methods in a variant and what the relationship is between methods of the same name in the different variants.
Correct. Let's do something about it. Take a close look at this visitor class.	[4] These methods look familiar. Have we seen them before?

```
class OnlyOnions^V {
  boolean forSkewer() {
    return true; }
  boolean forOnion(Shish^D s) {
    return s.onlyOnions(); }
  boolean forLamb(Shish^D s) {
    return false; }
  boolean forTomato(Shish^D s) {
    return false; }
}
```

$^\mathcal{V}$ This superscript is a reminder that the class is a visitor class. Lower superscripts when you enter this kind of definition in a file: `OnlyOnionsV`.

Almost. Each of them corresponds to an *onlyOnions* method in one of the variants of Shish$^\mathcal{D}$.	[5] That's right. The major difference is that they are all in one class, a visitor, whose name is OnlyOnions$^\mathcal{V}$.
Is *onlyOnions* different from OnlyOnions$^\mathcal{V}$?	[6] The former is used to name methods, the latter names a class.

And that's the whole point.	[7] What point?

We want all the methods in one class.	[8] What methods?

Those methods that would have the same name if we placed them into the variants of a datatype in one class.	[9] If we could do that, it would be much easier to understand what action these methods perform.

That's what we are about to do. We are going to separate the action from the datatype.	[10] It's about time.

What is the difference between the method *onlyOnions* in the Onion variant and the method *forOnion* in the visitor OnlyOnions$^{\mathcal{V}}$?	[11] Everything following **return** is the same.

Right. What is the difference?	[12] The difference is that *onlyOnions* in Onion is followed by () and that *forOnion* in OnlyOnions$^{\mathcal{V}}$ is followed by (Shish$^{\mathcal{D}}$ s).

Yes, that is the difference. Are the other *for* methods in OnlyOnions$^{\mathcal{V}}$ related to their counterparts in the same way?	[13] Indeed, they are.

It is time to discuss the boring part.	[14] What boring part?

The boring part tells us how to make all of this work.	[15] True, we still don't know how to make Shish$^{\mathcal{D}}$ and its variants work with this visitor class, which contains all the action.

Now take a look at this.

```
abstract class Shish^D {
  OnlyOnions^V ooFn = new OnlyOnions^V();
  abstract boolean onlyOnions();
}
```

```
class Skewer extends Shish^D {
  boolean onlyOnions() {
    return ooFn.forSkewer(); }
}
```

```
class Onion extends Shish^D {
  Shish^D s;
  Onion(Shish^D _s) {
    s = _s; }

  boolean onlyOnions() {
    return ooFn.forOnion(s); }
}
```

```
class Lamb extends Shish^D {
  Shish^D s;
  Lamb(Shish^D _s) {
    s = _s; }

  boolean onlyOnions() {
    return ooFn.forLamb(s); }
}
```

```
class Tomato extends Shish^D {
  Shish^D s;
  Tomato(Shish^D _s) {
    s = _s; }

  boolean onlyOnions() {
    return ooFn.forTomato(s); }
}
```

16 This is a strange set of definitions. All the *onlyOnions* methods in the variants look alike. Each of them uses an instance of OnlyOnions^V, which is created in the datatype, to invoke a *for* method with a matching name.

What does the *forOnion* method in Onion consume?	[17] If "consume" refers to what follows the name between parentheses, the method consumes *s*, which is the rest of the shish.
That's what "consumption" is all about. And what does the *forSkewer* method in Skewer consume?	[18] Nothing, because a skewer is the basis of a shish and therefore has no fields.
So what does the $(\mathsf{Shish}^{\mathcal{D}}\ s)$ mean in the definition of *forOnion*?	[19] It is always the rest of the shish, below the top layer, which is an onion. In other words, it is everything but the onion.
Very good. The notation $(\mathsf{Shish}^{\mathcal{D}}\ s)$ means that *forOnion* consumes a $\mathsf{Shish}^{\mathcal{D}}$ and that between { and }, *s* stands for that shish.	[20] That makes sense and explains *s.onlyOnions*().
Explain *s.onlyOnions*().	[21] Here are our words: "*s* is a $\mathsf{Shish}^{\mathcal{D}}$, and therefore *s.onlyOnions*() determines whether what is below the onion is also edible by an onion lover."
Explain *ooFn.forOnion*(*s*).	[22] You knew we wouldn't let you down: "*ooFn.forOnion* says that we want to use the method we just described. It consumes a $\mathsf{Shish}^{\mathcal{D}}$, and *s* is the $\mathsf{Shish}^{\mathcal{D}}$ that represents what is below the onion."

So what is the value of
new Onion(
  new Onion(
    new Skewer()))
.*onlyOnions*()?
	[23] It is still true.

And how do we determine that value with these new definitions?	[24] We start with the *onlyOnions* method in Onion, but it immediately uses the *forOnion* method on the rest of the shish.

Chapter 4

And what does the *forOnion* method do?	25 It checks whether the rest of this shish is edible by onion lovers.
How does it do that?	26 It uses the method *onlyOnions* on *s*.
Isn't that where we started from?	27 Yes, we're going round and round.
Welcome to the carousel.	28 Fortunately, the shish shrinks as it goes around, and when we get to the skewer we stop.
And then the ride is over and we know that for this example the answer is true.	29 That's exactly it.
Do we need to remember that we are on a carousel?	30 No! Now that we understand how the separation of data and action works, we only need to look at the action part to understand how things work.
Is one example enough?	31 No, let's look at some of the other actions on shishes and pizzas.
Let's look at *isVegetarian* next. Here is the beginning of the protocol.[1]	32 What about it?

```
abstract class Shish𝒟 {
  OnlyOnions𝒱 ooFn = new OnlyOnions𝒱();
  IsVegetarian𝒱 ivFn = new IsVegetarian𝒱();
  abstract boolean onlyOnions();
  abstract boolean isVegetarian();
}
```

---

[1] *The American Heritage Dictionary* defines protocol as "[t]he form of ceremony and etiquette observed by diplomats and heads of state." For us, a protocol is an agreement on how classes that specify a datatype and its variants interact with classes that realize functions on that datatype.

33 We must add two lines to each variant, and they are almost the same as those for *ooFn*.

```
class Skewer extends Shish𝒟 {
  boolean onlyOnions() {
    return ooFn.forSkewer(); }
  boolean isVegetarian() {
    return ivFn.forSkewer(); }
}
```

```
class Onion extends Shish𝒟 {
  Shish𝒟 s;
  Onion(Shish𝒟 _s) {
    s = _s; }
```

```
  boolean onlyOnions() {
    return ooFn.forOnion(s); }
  boolean isVegetarian() {
    return ivFn.forOnion(s); }
}
```

```
class Lamb extends Shish𝒟 {
  Shish𝒟 s;
  Lamb(Shish𝒟 _s) {
    s = _s; }
```

```
  boolean onlyOnions() {
    return ooFn.forLamb(s); }
  boolean isVegetarian() {
    return ivFn.forLamb(s); }
}
```

```
class Tomato extends Shish𝒟 {
  Shish𝒟 s;
  Tomato(Shish𝒟 _s) {
    s = _s; }
```

```
  boolean onlyOnions() {
    return ooFn.forTomato(s); }
  boolean isVegetarian() {
    return ivFn.forTomato(s); }
}
```

That's why we call this part boring.	[34] True, there's very little to think about. It could be done automatically.
How do we define the visitor?	[35] Does that refer to the class that contains the actions?
Yes, that one. Define the visitor.	[36] It is like OnlyOnions$^\mathcal{V}$ except for the method *forTomato*.

```
class IsVegetarian^V {
  boolean forSkewer() {
    return true; }
  boolean forOnion(Shish^D s) {
    return s.isVegetarian(); }
  boolean forLamb(Shish^D s) {
    return false; }
  boolean forTomato(Shish^D s) {
    return s.isVegetarian(); }
}
```

Are we moving fast?	[37] Yes, but there are only a few interesting parts. The protocol is always the same and boring; the visitor is always closely related to what we saw in chapter 2.
How about a tea break?	[38] Instead of coffee?

The Fourth Bit of Advice

When writing several functions for the same self-referential datatype, use visitor protocols so that all methods for a function can be found in a single class.

Is

   new Anchovy(
    new Olive(
     new Anchovy(
      new Cheese(
       new Crust())))))

a shish kebab?

39

No, it's a pizza.

$$\boxed{\textbf{abstract class } \text{Pizza}^{\mathcal{D}} \; \{\}}$$

$$\boxed{\textbf{class } \text{Crust } \textbf{extends } \text{Pizza}^{\mathcal{D}} \; \{\}}$$

$$\boxed{\begin{array}{l} \textbf{class } \text{Cheese } \textbf{extends } \text{Pizza}^{\mathcal{D}} \; \{ \\ \quad \text{Pizza}^{\mathcal{D}} \; p; \\ \quad \text{Cheese}(\text{Pizza}^{\mathcal{D}} \; \_p) \; \{ \\ \qquad p = \_p; \; \} \\ \\ \hline \\ \} \end{array}}$$

$$\boxed{\begin{array}{l} \textbf{class } \text{Olive } \textbf{extends } \text{Pizza}^{\mathcal{D}} \; \{ \\ \quad \text{Pizza}^{\mathcal{D}} \; p; \\ \quad \text{Olive}(\text{Pizza}^{\mathcal{D}} \; \_p) \; \{ \\ \qquad p = \_p; \; \} \\ \\ \hline \\ \} \end{array}}$$

$$\boxed{\begin{array}{l} \textbf{class } \text{Anchovy } \textbf{extends } \text{Pizza}^{\mathcal{D}} \; \{ \\ \quad \text{Pizza}^{\mathcal{D}} \; p; \\ \quad \text{Anchovy}(\text{Pizza}^{\mathcal{D}} \; \_p) \; \{ \\ \qquad p = \_p; \; \} \\ \\ \hline \\ \} \end{array}}$$

$$\boxed{\begin{array}{l} \textbf{class } \text{Sausage } \textbf{extends } \text{Pizza}^{\mathcal{D}} \; \{ \\ \quad \text{Pizza}^{\mathcal{D}} \; p; \\ \quad \text{Sausage}(\text{Pizza}^{\mathcal{D}} \; \_p) \; \{ \\ \qquad p = \_p; \; \} \\ \\ \hline \\ \} \end{array}}$$

So what do we do next?

We can define the protocol for the methods that belong to $\text{Pizza}^{\mathcal{D}}$ and its extensions: *remA*, *topAwC*, and *subAbC*.

Great! Here is the abstract portion of the protocol.

```
abstract class Pizza^D {
  RemA^V remFn = new RemA^V();
  TopAwC^V topFn = new TopAwC^V();
  SubAbC^V subFn = new SubAbC^V();
  abstract Pizza^D remA();
  abstract Pizza^D topAwC();
  abstract Pizza^D subAbC();
}
```

And here are some variants.

```
class Crust extends Pizza^D {
  Pizza^D remA() {
    return remFn.forCrust(); }
  Pizza^D topAwC() {
    return topFn.forCrust(); }
  Pizza^D subAbC() {
    return subFn.forCrust(); }
}
```

```
class Cheese extends Pizza^D {
  Pizza^D p;
  Cheese(Pizza^D _p) {
    p = _p; }

  Pizza^D remA() {
    return remFn.forCheese(p); }
  Pizza^D topAwC() {
    return topFn.forCheese(p); }
  Pizza^D subAbC() {
    return subFn.forCheese(p); }
}
```

Define the rest.

How innovative! The variants are totally mindless, now.

```
class Olive extends Pizza^D {
  Pizza^D p;
  Olive(Pizza^D _p) {
    p = _p; }

  Pizza^D remA() {
    return remFn.forOlive(p); }
  Pizza^D topAwC() {
    return topFn.forOlive(p); }
  Pizza^D subAbC() {
    return subFn.forOlive(p); }
}
```

```
class Anchovy extends Pizza^D {
  Pizza^D p;
  Anchovy(Pizza^D _p) {
    p = _p; }

  Pizza^D remA() {
    return remFn.forAnchovy(p); }
  Pizza^D topAwC() {
    return topFn.forAnchovy(p); }
  Pizza^D subAbC() {
    return subFn.forAnchovy(p); }
}
```

```
class Sausage extends Pizza^D {
  Pizza^D p;
  Sausage(Pizza^D _p) {
    p = _p; }

  Pizza^D remA() {
    return remFn.forSausage(p); }
  Pizza^D topAwC() {
    return topFn.forSausage(p); }
  Pizza^D subAbC() {
    return subFn.forSausage(p); }
}
```

We are all set.

Is it time to define the visitors that correspond to the methods $remA$, $topAwC$, and $subAbC$?

Okay, here is RemA$^\mathcal{V}$.

By now, even this is routine.

```
class RemA𝒱 {
  Pizza𝒟 forCrust() {
    return new Crust(); }
  Pizza𝒟 forCheese(Pizza𝒟 p) {
    return new Cheese(p.remA()); }
  Pizza𝒟 forOlive(Pizza𝒟 p) {
    return new Olive(p.remA()); }
  Pizza𝒟 forAnchovy(Pizza𝒟 p) {
    return p.remA(); }
  Pizza𝒟 forSausage(Pizza𝒟 p) {
    return new Sausage(p.remA()); }
}
```

```
class TopAwC𝒱 {
  Pizza𝒟 forCrust() {
    return new Crust(); }
  Pizza𝒟 forCheese(Pizza𝒟 p) {
    return new Cheese(p.topAwC()); }
  Pizza𝒟 forOlive(Pizza𝒟 p) {
    return new Olive(p.topAwC()); }
  Pizza𝒟 forAnchovy(Pizza𝒟 p) {
    return
      new Cheese(
        new Anchovy(p.topAwC())); }
  Pizza𝒟 forSausage(Pizza𝒟 p) {
    return new Sausage(p.topAwC()); }
}
```

Define TopAwC$^\mathcal{V}$.

The last one, SubAbC$^\mathcal{V}$, is a piece of cake.

44

And we thought we were working with a pizza pie.

```
class SubAbC𝒱 {
  Pizza𝒟 forCrust() {
    return new Crust(); }
  Pizza𝒟 forCheese(Pizza𝒟 p) {
    return new Cheese(p.subAbC()); }
  Pizza𝒟 forOlive(Pizza𝒟 p) {
    return new Olive(p.subAbC()); }
  Pizza𝒟 forAnchovy(Pizza𝒟 p) {
    return new Cheese(p.subAbC()); }
  Pizza𝒟 forSausage(Pizza𝒟 p) {
    return new Sausage(p.subAbC()); }
}
```

5.
Objects Are
People, Too

Have we seen this kind of definition before?[1]

```
abstract class Pie^D {
 ──── ( Pie ) ────
}
```

```
class Bot extends Pie^D {
 ──── ( Bot ) ────
}
```

```
class Top extends Pie^D {
  Object t;
  Pie^D r;
  Top(Object _t,Pie^D _r) {
    t = _t;
    r = _r; }
 ───────────────────────────
 ──── ( Top ) ────
}
```

---

[1] Better names for these classes would be `PizzaPieD`, `Bottom` and `Topping`, respectively.

What? More pizza!

Yes, still more pizza, but this one is different.

Yes, it includes only one variant for adding toppings to a pizza, and toppings are Objects.

What kind of toppings can we put on these kinds of pizza?

Any kind, because Object is the class of all objects. Here are some fish toppings.

```
abstract class Fish^D {}
```

```
class Anchovy extends Fish^D {}
```

```
class Salmon extends Fish^D {}
```

```
class Tuna extends Fish^D {}
```

Nice datatype. Is
  new Top(**new** Anchovy(),
    new Top(**new** Tuna(),
      new Top(**new** Anchovy(),
        new Bot()))))
a pizza pie?

4 It is a pizza pie, and so is
  new Top(**new** Tuna(),
    new Top(**new** Integer(42),
      new Top(**new** Anchovy(),
        new Top(**new** Integer(5),
          new Bot())))).

What is the value of
  new Top(**new** Salmon(),
    new Top(**new** Anchovy(),
      new Top(**new** Tuna(),
        new Top(**new** Anchovy(),
          new Bot()))))
  .remA()?

5 It is this fishy pizza pie:
  new Top(**new** Salmon(),
    new Top(**new** Tuna(),
      new Bot())).

Is it true that the value of
  new Top(**new** Salmon(),
    new Top(**new** Tuna(),
      new Bot()))
  .remA()

is
  new Top(**new** Salmon(),
    new Top(**new** Tuna(),
      new Bot()))?

6 Yes. The pizza that comes out is the same as the one that goes in, because there are no anchovies on that pizza.

Does *remA* belong to Pie$^\mathcal{D}$?

7 Yes, and it produces pizza pies.

Define the protocol for RemA$^\mathcal{V}$. We provide the **abstract** part.

RemA$^\mathcal{V}$ *raFn* = **new** RemA$^\mathcal{V}$();
abstract Pie$^\mathcal{D}$ *remA*();

                        Pie

8 This is easy by now.

Pie$^\mathcal{D}$ *remA*() {
  return *raFn.forBot*(); }

                        Bot

Pie$^\mathcal{D}$ *remA*() {
  return *raFn.forTop*(*t*,*r*); }

                        Top

Great. Isn't that easy?	[9] Easy and boring.

What part of this exercise differs from datatype to datatype?	[10] Determining how many fields a variant contains. In our case, we had zero and two.

Anything else?	[11] No, from that we know that *raFn.forBot* is followed by () and *raFn.forTop* by (t,r).

Why (t,r)?	[12] Because these are the fields of Top.

Let's define the visitor RemA$^{\mathcal{V}}$.

[13] Here are some guesses.

```
class RemA^V {
  Pie^D forBot() {
    return _____ ; }
  Pie^D forTop(Object t,Pie^D r) {
    if (new Anchovy().equals(t))
      return _____ ;
    else
      return _____ ; }
}
```

```
class RemA^V {
  Pie^D forBot() {
    return new Bot(); }
  Pie^D forTop(Object t,Pie^D r) {
    if (new Anchovy().equals(t))
      return r.remA();
    else
      return new Top(t,r.remA()); }
}
```

Great guesses! What does
```
if (expr_1)
  return expr_2;
else
  return expr_3;
```
mean?

[14] We guess:
"This produces the value of either $expr_2$ or $expr_3$, depending on whether or not $expr_1$ is determined to be true or false, respectively."

And what does
new Anchovy().*equals*(t)
mean?

[15] We could guess:
"This expression determines whether t is equal to **new** Anchovy()."

Not yet. It depends on what *equals* means.	[16] What?

What is the value of
  new Anchovy().*equals*(**new** Anchovy())?

[17] The "Not yet." implies that the value is false.

Yes! And what is the value of
  new Anchovy().*equals*(**new** Tuna())?

[18] false,
   because no anchovy is a tuna.

The class Object contains a method called *equals*. This method compares one Object to another, and it always returns false.[1]

_____

[1] Not always, We explain the correct answer in chapter 10.

[19] If we know that *equals*'s answer is always false, why bother to use it?

We must define it anew[1] for all classes whose instances we wish to compare.

_____

[1] In Java, redefining a method is called "overriding."

[20] Okay. How?

For Fish$^{\mathcal{D}}$ and its variants it works like this.

```
abstract class Fish^D {}
```

```
class Anchovy extends Fish^D {
  public^1 boolean equals(Object o) {
    return (o instanceof Anchovy); }
}
```

```
class Salmon extends Fish^D {
  public boolean equals(Object o) {
    return (o instanceof Salmon); }
}
```

```
class Tuna extends Fish^D {
  public boolean equals(Object o) {
    return (o instanceof Tuna); }
}
```

[21] Assuming that
   (*o* **instanceof** Tuna)
is true when *o* is an instance of Tuna, these method definitions are obvious.

_____

[1] The class Object is defined in a separate package, called java.lang.Object. Overriding methods that reside in other packages requires the word public.

Aren't they? Is every value constructed with **new** an instance of Object? ²²

Yes. Every such value is an Object, because every class **extends** Object directly or indirectly.

If **class** A **extends** B, is every value created by **new** $A(\dots)$ an instance of class B? ²³

Yes, and of the class that B extends and so on.

Now, what is the value of

  new Anchovy().*equals*(**new** Anchovy())? ²⁴

true,

  because **new** Anchovy() is an instance of Anchovy.

Yet the value of

  new Anchovy().*equals*(**new** Tuna())

is still false. ²⁵

Of course, because an anchovy is never a tuna.

Could we have written RemA$^\mathcal{V}$ without using *equals*? ²⁶

Absolutely, **instanceof** is enough.

```
class RemAᵛ {
  Pieᴰ forBot() {
    return new Bot(); }
  Pieᴰ forTop(Object t,Pieᴰ r) {
    if (t instanceof Anchovy)
      return r.remA();
    else
      return new Top(t,r.remA()); }
}
```

Why haven't we defined it this way?

Easy, because we want to generalize RemA$^\mathcal{V}$ so that it works for any kind of fish topping. ²⁷

We can do that, but when we use the methods of the more general visitor, we need to say which kind of fish we want to remove.

What are good names for the more general methods and visitor? ²⁸

How about *remFish* and RemFish$^\mathcal{V}$?

How do we use *remFish*?

29

We give it a $\mathsf{Fish}^{\mathcal{D}}$.

Add the protocol for $\mathsf{RemFish}^{\mathcal{V}}$. We designed the abstract portion.

> $\mathsf{RemFish}^{\mathcal{V}}$ *rfFn* = **new** $\mathsf{RemFish}^{\mathcal{V}}$();
> **abstract** $\mathsf{Pie}^{\mathcal{D}}$ *remFish*($\mathsf{Fish}^{\mathcal{D}}$ *f*);
>
> Pie

The rest is routine.

> $\mathsf{Pie}^{\mathcal{D}}$ *remFish*($\mathsf{Fish}^{\mathcal{D}}$ *f*) {
>   **return** *rfFn.forBot*(*f*); }
>
> Bot

> $\mathsf{Pie}^{\mathcal{D}}$ *remFish*($\mathsf{Fish}^{\mathcal{D}}$ *f*) {
>   **return** *rfFn.forTop*(*t*,*r*,*f*); }
>
> Top

Where do (*f*) and (*t*,*r*,*f*) come from?

The *f* stands for the $\mathsf{Fish}^{\mathcal{D}}$ we want to remove in both cases. The *t* and the *r* are the fields of Top; Bot doesn't have any.

Let's define $\mathsf{RemFish}^{\mathcal{V}}$ and its two methods.

Instead of comparing the top layer *t* of the pizza to $\mathsf{Anchovy}$, we now determine whether it equals the $\mathsf{Fish}^{\mathcal{D}}$ *f*, which is the additional value consumed by the method.

> **class** $\mathsf{RemFish}^{\mathcal{V}}$ {
> $\mathsf{Pie}^{\mathcal{D}}$ *forBot*($\mathsf{Fish}^{\mathcal{D}}$ *f*) {
>   **return new** Bot(); }
> $\mathsf{Pie}^{\mathcal{D}}$ *forTop*(Object *t*,$\mathsf{Pie}^{\mathcal{D}}$ *r*,$\mathsf{Fish}^{\mathcal{D}}$ *f*) {
>   **if** (*f.equals*(*t*))
>   **return** *r.remFish*(*f*);
>   **else**
>   **return new** Top(*t*,*r.remFish*(*f*)); }
> }

If we add another kind of fish to our datatype, what would happen to the definition of $\mathsf{RemFish}^{\mathcal{V}}$?

33

Nothing, we just have to remember to add *equals* to the new variant.

Let's try it out with a short example:
  new Top(**new** Anchovy(),
    new Bot())
  .*remFish*(**new** Anchovy()).

34 The object is a topping, so we use *forTop* from RemFish$^{\mathcal{V}}$.

Yes. What values does *forTop* consume?

35 It consumes three values: **new** Anchovy(), which is t, the top-most layer of the pizza; **new** Bot(), which is r, the rest of the pizza; and **new** Anchovy(), which is f, the Fish$^{\mathcal{D}}$ to be removed.

And now?

36 Now we need to determine the value of
  if ($f.equals(t)$)
    return $r.remFish(f)$;
  else
    return new Top(t,$r.remFish(f)$);
where t, r, and f stand for the values just mentioned.

So?

37 Given what f and t stand for, $f.equals(t)$ is true. Hence, we must determine the value of $r.remFish(f)$.

What is the value of
  new Bot()
  .*remFish*(**new** Anchovy())?

38 It is the same as
  forBot(f),
where f is **new** Anchovy().

What does *forBot* in RemFish$^{\mathcal{V}}$ produce?

39 It produces **new** Bot(), no matter what f is.

All clear?

40 Ready to move on, after snack time.

Does
  new Top(**new** Integer(2),
   new Top(**new** Integer(3),
    new Top(**new** Integer(2),
     new Bot())))
  .*remInt*(**new** Integer(3))
look familiar?

[41] Yes, it looks like what we just evaluated.

What does *remInt* do?

[42] It removes Integers from pizza pies just as *remFish* removes fish from pizza pies.

Who defined *equals* for Integer?

[43] The Machine decided
    new Integer(0).*equals*(**new** Integer(0))
to be true, and the rest was obvious.

Define the visitor RemInt$^{\mathcal{V}}$.

[44] Wonderful! We do the interesting thing first. This visitor is almost identical to RemFish$^{\mathcal{V}}$. We just need to change the type of what the two methods consume.

```
class RemInt^V {
  Pie^D forBot(Integer i) {
    return new Bot(); }
  Pie^D forTop(Object t,Pie^D r,Integer i) {
    if (i.equals(t))
      return r.remInt(i);
    else
      return new Top(t,r.remInt(i)); }
}
```

Does it matter that this definition uses i and not f?

[45] No, i is just a better name than f, no other reason. As long as we do such substitutions systematically, we are just fine.

Where is the protocol?

[46] It is so simple, let's save it for later.

Can we remove Integers from $\text{Pie}^{\mathcal{D}}$s?	[47] Yes.

Can we remove $\text{Fish}^{\mathcal{D}}$ from $\text{Pie}^{\mathcal{D}}$s?	[48] Yes, and we use nearly identical definitions.

Let's combine the two definitions.	[49] If we use Object instead of the underlined Integer above, everything works out.

Why?	[50] Because everything constructed with **new** is an Object.

Just do it!	[51] It's done.

```
class Rem^V {
  Pie^D forBot(Object o) {
    return new Bot(); }
  Pie^D forTop(Object t,Pie^D r,Object o) {
    if (o.equals(t))
      return r.rem(o);
    else
      return new Top(t,r.rem(o)); }
}
```

Should we do the protocol for all these visitors?	[52] Now?

You never know when it might be useful, even if it does not contain any interesting information.	[53] Let's just consider Rem^V.

Why not RemFish^V and RemA^V and RemInt^V?	[54] They are unnecessary once we have Rem^V.

Here is the **abstract** portion of Pie$^\mathcal{D}$.

```
abstract class Pie^D {
  Rem^V remFn = new Rem^V();
  abstract Pie^D rem(Object o);
}
```

And here are the pieces for Bot and Top.

```
class Bot extends Pie^D {
  Pie^D rem(Object o) {
    return remFn.forBot(o); }
}
```

```
class Top extends Pie^D {
  Object t;
  Pie^D r;
  Top(Object _t,Pie^D _r) {
    t = _t;
    r = _r; }

  Pie^D rem(Object o) {
    return remFn.forTop(t,r,o); }
}
```

Let's remove some things from pizza pies:
```
    new Top(new Integer(2),
      new Top(new Integer(3),
        new Top(new Integer(2),
          new Bot())))
  .rem(new Integer(3)).
```

Works like a charm with the same result as before.

And how about
```
    new Top(new Anchovy(),
      new Bot())
  .rem(new Anchovy())?
```

Ditto.

Next:
```
    new Top(new Anchovy(),
      new Top(new Integer(3),
        new Top(new Zero(),
          new Bot())))
  .rem(new Integer(3)).
```

No problem. This, too, removes **3** and leaves the other layers alone:
```
      new Top(new Anchovy(),
        new Top(new Zero(),
          new Bot())).
```

What is the value of
  new Top(**new** Anchovy(),
    new Top(**new** Integer(3),
      new Top(**new** Zero(),
        new Bot()))))
.*rem*(**new** Zero())?

59 Oops. The answer is
    new Top(**new** Anchovy(),
      new Top(**new** Integer(3),
        new Top(**new** Zero(),
          new Bot())))).

What's wrong with that?

60 We expected it to remove **new** Zero() from the pizza.

And why didn't it?

61 Because *equals* for $\text{Num}^{\mathcal{D}}$s uses Object's *equals*, which always produces false—as we discussed above when we introduced *equals*.

Always?

62 Unless we define it anew for those classes whose instances we wish to compare.

Here is the version of $\text{Num}^{\mathcal{D}}$ (including OneMoreThan) with its own *equals*. Define the new Zero variant.

```
abstract class Num^D {}
```

```
class OneMoreThan extends Num^D {
  Num^D predecessor;
  OneMoreThan(Num^D _p) {
    predecessor = _p; }

  public boolean equals(Object o) {
    if (o instanceof OneMoreThan)
      return
        predecessor
        .equals(
          ((OneMoreThan)o)^1.predecessor);
    else
      return false; }
}
```

63 Adding *equals* to Zero is easy. We use **instanceof** to determine whether the consumed value is a **new** Zero().

```
class Zero extends Num^D {
  public boolean equals(Object o) {
    return (o instanceof Zero); }
}
```

But what is the underlining of
  ((OneMoreThan)*o*)
about? Wouldn't it have been sufficient to write *o.predecessor*?

---

[1] In Java, this is called (downward) casting, because `OneMoreThan` extends `NumD`.

ιe type of *o*?	64 Object, according to (Object *o*), which is what declares the type of *o*.
So what is *o.predecessor*?	65 Nonsense.
Correct. What do we know after **if** has determined that (*o* **instanceof** OneMoreThan) is **true**?	66 We know that *o*'s type is Object and that it is an instance of OneMoreThan.
Precisely. So what does ((OneMoreThan)*o*) do?	67 It converts the type of *o* from Object to OneMoreThan.
What is ((OneMoreThan) *o*)'s type?	68 Its type is OneMoreThan, and now it makes sense to write ((OneMoreThan) *o*).*predecessor*.
Are *o* and ((OneMoreThan)*o*) interchangeable?	69 The underlying object is the same. But no, the two expressions are not interchangeable, because the former's type is Object, whereas the latter's is OneMoreThan.
Is this complicated?	70 Someone has been drinking too much coffee.

Did you also notice the
  predecessor
  .*equals*(
    ((OneMoreThan)*o*).*predecessor*)
in *equals* for OneMoreThan?
	71 How do the two uses of *predecessor* differ?

The first one, *predecessor*, refers to the *predecessor* field of the instance of OneMoreThan on which we are using *equals*. And that field might not be a OneMoreThan.	72 So the second one, ((OneMoreThan) *o*).*predecessor*, refers to the *predecessor* field of the instance of OneMoreThan consumed by *equals*.

Yes. Are these two objects equal?

73 If they are similar[1] to the same **int**, they are equal. But most of the time, they are not.

---
[1] Check chapter 1 for "similar."

Time for lunch?

74 That's just in time.

Did you have a good lunch break?

75 Yes, thank you.

Now what is the value of
  new Top(**new** Anchovy(),
    new Top(**new** Integer(3),
      new Top(**new** Zero(),
        new Bot())))
  .*rem*(**new** Zero())?

76 Now we get
  new Top(**new** Anchovy(),
    new Top(**new** Integer(3),
      new Bot())),
which is precisely what we want.

And why?

77 Because *equals* now knows how to compare Num$^\mathcal{D}$s.

Do we always add *equals* to a class?

78 No, only if we need it.

Do we need *equals* when we want to substitute one item for another on a pizza pie?

79 Yes, we do.

What is the value of
  new Top(**new** Anchovy(),
    new Top(**new** Tuna(),
      new Top(**new** Anchovy(),
        new Bot())))
  .*substFish*(**new** Salmon(),
        new Anchovy())?

80 It is the same pizza pie with all the anchovies replaced by salmon:
  new Top(**new** Salmon(),
    new Top(**new** Tuna(),
      new Top(**new** Salmon(),
        new Bot())))).

What kind of values does *substFish* consume? 81 It consumes two *fish* and works on Pie$^\mathcal{D}$s.

Objects Are People, Too

And what does it produce?

82

It always produces a Pie$^{\mathcal{D}}$.

What is the value of
  new Top(new Integer(3),
    new Top(new Integer(2),
      new Top(new Integer(3),
       new Bot()))))
  .*substInt*(new Integer(5),
         new Integer(3))?

83

It is the same pizza pie with all 3s replaced by 5s:
  new Top(new Integer(5),
    new Top(new Integer(2),
      new Top(new Integer(5),
       new Bot()))).

What kind of values does *substInt* consume?

84

It consumes two Integers and works on Pie$^{\mathcal{D}}$s.

And what does it produce?

85

It always produces a Pie$^{\mathcal{D}}$.

We can define SubstFish$^{\mathcal{V}}$.

```
class SubstFishⱽ {
  Pieᴰ forBot(Fishᴰ n,Fishᴰ o) {
    return new Bot(); }
  Pieᴰ forTop(Object t,
              Pieᴰ r,
              Fishᴰ n,
              Fishᴰ o) {
    if (o.equals(t))
      return new Top(n,r.substFish(n,o));
    else
      return new Top(t,r.substFish(n,o)); }
}
```

Define SubstInt$^{\mathcal{V}}$.

86

To get from SubstFish$^{\mathcal{V}}$ to SubstInt$^{\mathcal{V}}$, we just need to substitute Fish$^{\mathcal{D}}$ by Integer everywhere and 'Fish" by "Int" in the class and method names.

```
class SubstIntⱽ {
  Pieᴰ forBot(Integer n,Integer o) {
    return new Bot(); }
  Pieᴰ forTop(Object t,
              Pieᴰ r,
              Integer n,
              Integer o) {
    if (o.equals(t))
      return new Top(n,r.substInt(n,o));
    else
      return new Top(t,r.substInt(n,o)); }
}
```

Did we forget the boring parts?

87

Yes, because there is obviously a more general version like Rem$^{\mathcal{V}}$.

Yes, we call it $\mathsf{Subst}^{\mathcal{V}}$. Define it.

We substitute Object for $\mathsf{Fish}^{\mathcal{D}}$ and $\mathsf{Integer}$.

```
class Subst^V {
  Pie^D forBot(Object n,Object o) {
    return new Bot(); }
  Pie^D forTop(Object t,
               Pie^D r,
               Object n,
               Object o) {
  if (o.equals(t))
    return new Top(n,r.subst(n,o));
  else
    return new Top(t,r.subst(n,o)); }
}
```

Now it is time to add the protocol for $\mathsf{Subst}^{\mathcal{V}}$ to $\mathsf{Pie}^{\mathcal{D}}$. Here are the variants.

```
class Bot extends Pie^D {
  Pie^D rem(Object o) {
    return remFn.forBot(o); }
  Pie^D subst(Object n,Object o) {
    return substFn.forBot(n,o); }
}
```

```
class Top extends Pie^D {
  Object t;
  Pie^D r;
  Top(Object _t,Pie^D _r) {
    t = _t;
    r = _r; }

  Pie^D rem(Object o) {
    return remFn.forTop(t,r,o); }
  Pie^D subst(Object n,Object o) {
    return substFn.forTop(t,r,n,o); }
}
```

The abstract part is obvious.

```
abstract class Pie^D {
  Rem^V remFn = new Rem^V();
  Subst^V substFn = new Subst^V();
  abstract Pie^D rem(Object o);
  abstract Pie^D subst(Object n,Object o);
}
```

So?

That was some heavy lifting.

Objects Are People, Too

6.
Boring Protocols

Are protocols truly boring?

¹ We acted as if they were.

But, of course they are not. We just didn't want to spend much time on them. Let's take a closer look at the last one we defined in the previous chapter.

```
abstract class Pie^D {
  Rem^V remFn = new Rem^V();
  Subst^V substFn = new Subst^V();
  abstract Pie^D rem(Object o);
  abstract Pie^D subst(Object n,Object o);
}
```

² Okay, here are the variants again.

```
class Bot extends Pie^D {
  Pie^D rem(Object o) {
    return remFn.forBot(o); }
  Pie^D subst(Object n,Object o) {
    return substFn.forBot(n,o); }
}
```

```
class Top extends Pie^D {
  Object t;
  Pie^D r;
  Top(Object _t,Pie^D _r) {
    t = _t;
    r = _r; }

  Pie^D rem(Object o) {
    return remFn.forTop(t,r,o); }
  Pie^D subst(Object n,Object o) {
    return substFn.forTop(t,r,n,o); }
}
```

What is the difference between *rem* and *subst* in Pie^D?

³ The first one consumes one Object, the second one consumes two.

What is the difference between *rem* and *subst* in the Bot variant?

⁴ Simple: *rem* asks for the *forBot* service from *remFn* and hands over the Object it consumes; *subst* asks for the *forBot* service from *substFn* and hands over the two Objects it consumes.

What is the difference between *rem* and *subst* in the Top variant?

⁵ Simpler: *rem* asks for the *forTop* service from *remFn* and hands over the field values and the Object it consumes; *subst* asks for the *forTop* service from *substFn* and hands over the field values and the two Objects it consumes.

And that is all there is to the methods in the variants of a protocol.[6]

But $remFn$ and $substFn$ defined in the datatype are still a bit mysterious.

Let's not create $remFn$ and $substFn$ in the datatype.[7]

```
abstract class Pie𝒟 {
  abstract Pie𝒟 rem(Rem𝒱 remFn,
                     Object o);
  abstract Pie𝒟 subst(Subst𝒱 substFn,
                       Object n,
                       Object o);
}
```

This looks like an obvious modification. The new rem and $subst$ now consume a $remFn$ and a $substFn$, respectively. Can they still find $forBot$ and $forTop$, their corresponding carousel partners?

Yes, it is a straightforward trade-off. Instead of adding a $remFn$ field and a $substFn$ field to the datatype, we now have rem or $subst$ consume such values. What kind of values are consumed by rem and $subst$?[8]

The definition of the datatype says that they are a Rem𝒱 and a Subst𝒱, respectively. And every Rem𝒱 defines $forBot$ and $forTop$, and so does every Subst𝒱.

Here is how it changes Top.[9]

```
class Top extends Pie𝒟 {
  Object t;
  Pie𝒟 r;
  Top(Object _t,Pie𝒟 _r) {
    t = _t;
    r = _r; }

  Pie𝒟 rem(Rem𝒱 remFn,
           Object o) {
    return remFn.forTop(t,r,o); }
  Pie𝒟 subst(Subst𝒱 substFn,
             Object n,
             Object o) {
    return substFn.forTop(t,r,n,o); }
}
```

How does it affect Bot?

In the same manner. We just need to change each concrete method's description of what it consumes. The rest remains the same.

```
class Bot extends Pie𝒟 {
  Pie𝒟 rem(Rem𝒱 remFn,
           Object o) {
    return remFn.forBot(o); }
  Pie𝒟 subst(Subst𝒱 substFn,
             Object n,
             Object o) {
    return substFn.forBot(n,o); }
}
```

That's right. Nothing else changes in the variants. Instead of relying on fields of the datatype, we use what is consumed.

10 We still have some work to do.

Like what?

11 Consuming an extra value here also affects how the methods *rem* and *subst* are used.

Where are they used?

12 In Rem$^\mathcal{V}$ and Subst$^\mathcal{V}$, the interesting parts, for example.

Yes. Here is Rem$^\mathcal{V}$.

13 That takes all the fun out of it.

```
class Rem^D {
  Pie^D forBot(Object o) {
    return new Bot(); }
  Pie^D forTop(Object t,
               Pie^D r,
               Object o) {
    if (o.equals(t))
      return r.rem(this,o);
    else
      return new Top(t,r.rem(this,o)); }
}
```

Modify Subst$^\mathcal{V}$ accordingly.

```
class Subst^D {
  Pie^D forBot(Object n,
               Object o) {
    return new Bot(); }
  Pie^D forTop(Object t,
               Pie^D r,
               Object n,
               Object o) {
    if (o.equals(t))
      return
        new Top(n,r.subst(this,n,o));
    else
      return
        new Top(t,r.subst(this,n,o)); }
}
```

What is **this** all about?

14 Yes, what about it. Copying is easy.

Understanding is more difficult. The word **this** refers to the object itself.

15 Which object?

How did we get here?

16 The protocol is that *rem* in Bot and Top asks for the *forBot* and *forTop* methods of *remFn*, respectively.

How does that happen?	[17] It happens with
	    $remFn.forBot(\ldots)$
	and
	    $remFn.forTop(\ldots)$,
	respectively.

Correct. And now *forBot* and *forTop* can refer to the object *remFn* as **this**.	[18] Oh, so inside the methods of $Rem^\mathcal{V}$, **this** stands for precisely that instance of $Rem^\mathcal{V}$ that allowed us to use those methods in the first place. And that must mean that when we use $r.rem(\textbf{this},\ldots)$ in *forTop*, it tells *rem* to use the same instance over again.

That's it. Tricky?	[19] Not really, just self-referential.

Why?	[20] Because **this** is a $Rem^\mathcal{V}$, and it is exactly what we need to complete the job.

What is the value of
  new Top(**new** Anchovy(),
    new Top(**new** Integer(3),
    new Top(**new** Zero(),
    new Bot())))
 .*rem*(<u>**new** Rem$^\mathcal{V}$()</u>,
   new Zero())?
	[21] We did the same example in the preceding chapter, and the result remains the same.

And how does the underlined part relate to what we did there?	[22] It creates a $Rem^\mathcal{V}$ object, which corresponds to the *remFn* in the old $Pie^\mathcal{D}$.

What is the value of
  new Top(**new** Integer(3),
    new Top(**new** Integer(2),
    new Top(**new** Integer(3),
    new Bot())))
 .*subst*(<u>**new** Subst$^\mathcal{V}$()</u>,
   <u>**new** Integer(5)</u>,
   new Integer(3))?
	[23] We did the same example in the preceding chapter, and the result remains the same.

And how does the underlined part relate to what we did there?	24 It creates a $\mathsf{Subst}^{\mathcal{V}}$ object, which corresponds to the *remFn* in the old $\mathsf{Pie}^{\mathcal{D}}$.
So what is the underlined part about?	25 We changed the methods in $\mathsf{Pie}^{\mathcal{D}}$, which means that we must also change how it is used.
Ready for the next protocol?	26 Let's grab a quick snack.
How about some ice cream?	27 Cappuccino crunch sounds great. The more coffee, the better.
Take a look at *subst* in Top and at *forTop* in $\mathsf{Subst}^{\mathcal{V}}$. What happens to the values that they consume?	28 Nothing really. They get handed back and forth, though *forTop* compares *o* to *t*.
Is the handing back and forth necessary?	29 We don't know any better way, yet.
Here is a way to define $\mathsf{Subst}^{\mathcal{V}}$ that avoids the handing back and forth of these extra values.	30 Wow. This visitor has two fields.[1]

```
class Substᵛ {
  Object n;
  Object o;
  Substᵛ(Object _n,Object _o) {
    n = _n;
    o = _o; }

  Pieᴰ forBot() {
    return new Bot(); }
  Pieᴰ forTop(Object t,Pieᴰ r) {
    if (o.equals(t))
      return new Top(n,r.subst(this));
    else
      return new Top(t,r.subst(this)); }
}
```

[1] In functional programming, a visitor with fields is called a closure (or a higher-order function), which would be the result of applying a curried version of subst.

How do we create a Subst$^\mathcal{V}$?

31 We use
$$\text{\textbf{new} Subst}^\mathcal{V}(\textbf{new Integer}(5),$$
$$\textbf{new Integer}(3)).$$

What does that do?

32 It creates a Subst$^\mathcal{V}$ whose methods know how to substitute **new Integer**(5) for all occurrences of **new Integer**(3) in Pie$^\mathcal{D}$.

How do the methods know that without consuming more values?

33 The values have now become fields of the Subst$^\mathcal{V}$ object to which the methods belong. They no longer need to be consumed.

Okay, so how would we *subst*itute all **new** Integer(3) with **new** Integer(5) in
   new Top(**new** Integer(3),
    new Top(**new** Integer(2),
     new Top(**new** Integer(3),
      new Bot()))))?

34 We write
  new Top(**new** Integer(3),
   new Top(**new** Integer(2),
    new Top(**new** Integer(3),
     new Bot())))
  .*subst*(**new** Subst$^\mathcal{V}$(
      new Integer(5),
      new Integer(3))).

And if we want to *subst*itute all **new** Integer(2) with **new** Integer(7) in the same pie?

35 We write
  new Top(**new** Integer(3),
   new Top(**new** Integer(2),
    new Top(**new** Integer(3),
     new Bot())))
  .*subst*(**new** Subst$^\mathcal{V}$(
      new Integer(7),
      new Integer(2))).

Does all that mean we have to change the protocol, too?

36 Of course, because the methods *subst* in the Bot and Top variants consume only one value now.

Chapter 6

That's right. Here are the datatype and its Bot variant. Define the Top variant.

```
abstract class Pie𝒟 {
  abstract Pie𝒟 rem(Rem𝒱 remFn);
  abstract Pie𝒟 subst(Subst𝒱 substFn);
}
```

```
class Bot extends Pie𝒟 {
  Pie𝒟 rem(Rem𝒱 remFn) {
    return remFn.forBot(); }
  Pie𝒟 subst(Subst𝒱 substFn) {
    return substFn.forBot(); }
}
```

Is there anything else missing?

What is the difference between *rem* and *subst* in Bot?

What is the difference between *rem* and *subst* in Top?

Can we eliminate the differences?

True, because *substFn* is just a name for a value we don't know yet. But how can we make the types the same?

---

37 In the Top variant, we still need to hand over both t and r.

```
class Top extends Pie𝒟 {
  Object t;
  Pie𝒟 r;
  Top(Object _t,Pie𝒟 _r) {
    t = _t;
    r = _r; }

  Pie𝒟 rem(Rem𝒱 remFn) {
    return remFn.forTop(t,r); }
  Pie𝒟 subst(Subst𝒱 substFn) {
    return substFn.forTop(t,r); }
}
```

38 We haven't defined Rem𝒱 for this new protocol. But it is simple and hardly worth our attention.

39 Not much. The name of the respective values they consume and the corresponding types.

40 Not much. The name of the respective values they consume and the corresponding types.

41 It is easy to make them use the same names. It doesn't matter whether *rem* is defined as it is or as
```
  Pie𝒟 rem(Rem𝒱 substFn) {
    return substFn.forTop(t,r); }.
```

42 Both Rem𝒱 and Subst𝒱 are visitors that contain the same method names and those methods consume and produce the same types of values. We can think of them as extensions of a common **abstract class**.

Yes! Do it!

43

Here it is.

> **abstract class** PieVisitor$^{\mathcal{D}}$ {
>   **abstract** Pie$^{\mathcal{D}}$ *forBot*();
>   **abstract** Pie$^{\mathcal{D}}$ *forTop*(Object *t*,Pie$^{\mathcal{D}}$ *r*);
> }

Great job, except that we will use **interface** for specifying visitors like these.

> **interface** PieVisitor$^{\mathcal{I}}$ {
>   Pie$^{\mathcal{D}}$ *forBot*();
>   Pie$^{\mathcal{D}}$ *forTop*(Object *t*,Pie$^{\mathcal{D}}$ *r*);
> }

$^{\mathcal{I}}$ This superscript is a reminder that the name refers to an interface. Lower superscripts when you enter this kind of definition in a file: `PieVisitorI`.

Okay, that doesn't seem to be a great difference. Can a class extend an **interface** the way it **extends** an **abstract class**?

No. A class **implements** an **interface**; it does not extend it.

Fine.

Now that we have an interface that describes the type of the values consumed by *rem* and *subst*, can we make their definitions even more similar?

Yes, we can. Assuming we can use **interface**s like **abstract class**es, we can write
> Pie$^{\mathcal{D}}$ *rem*(PieVisitor$^{\mathcal{I}}$ *pvFn*) {
>   **return** *pvFn.forTop*(*t*,*r*); }

and
> Pie$^{\mathcal{D}}$ *subst*(PieVisitor$^{\mathcal{I}}$ *pvFn*) {
>   **return** *pvFn.forTop*(*t*,*r*); }

in Top.

Correct. What is the difference between *rem* and *subst*, now?

There isn't any. We can use the same name for both, as long as we remember to use it whenever we would have used *rem* or *subst*.

What is a good name for this method?

The method accepts a visitor and asks for its services, so we call it *accept*.

And what is a better name for *pvFn*?

Easy: *ask*, because we ask for services.

Now we can simplify the protocol. Here is the new Rem$^\mathcal{V}$.

```
class Rem^V implements PieVisitor^I {
  Object o;
  Rem^V(Object _o) {
   o = _o; }
  _____

  public Pie^D forBot() {
   return new Bot(); }
  public Pie^D forTop(Object t,Pie^D r) {
   if (o.equals(t))
    return r.accept(this);
   else
    return new Top(t,r.accept(this)); }
}
```

Supply the protocol.

Here we go.

```
abstract class Pie^D {
  abstract Pie^D accept(PieVisitor^I ask);
}
```

```
class Bot extends Pie^D {
  Pie^D accept(PieVisitor^I ask) {
   return ask.forBot(); }
}
```

```
class Top extends Pie^D {
  Object t;
  Pie^D r;
  Top(Object _t,Pie^D _r) {
   t = _t;
   r = _r; }
  _____

  Pie^D accept(PieVisitor^I ask) {
   return ask.forTop(t,r); }
}
```

Did you notice the two underlined occurrences of **public**?

Yes, what about them?

When we define a **class** that **implements** an **interface**, we need to add the word **public** to the left of the method definitions.

Why?

It's a way to say that these are the methods that satisfy the obligations imposed by the **interface**.

Looks weird, but let's move on.

Correct. They are just icing.

Okay, we still won't forget them.

Now define the new Subst$^\mathcal{V}$.

55 Here it is.

```
class Subst𝒱 implements PieVisitor𝐼 {
  Object n;
  Object o;
  Subst𝒱(Object _n,Object _o) {
    n = _n;
    o = _o; }
```
```
  public Pie𝒟 forBot() {
    return new Bot(); }
  public Pie𝒟 forTop(Object t,Pie𝒟 r) {
    if (o.equals(t))
      return
        new Top(n,r.accept(this));
    else
      return
        new Top(t,r.accept(this)); }
}
```

Draw a picture of the interface PieVisitor$^\mathcal{I}$ and all the classes: Pie$^\mathcal{D}$, Bot, Top, Rem$^\mathcal{V}$, and Subst$^\mathcal{V}$.

56 Here is our picture.

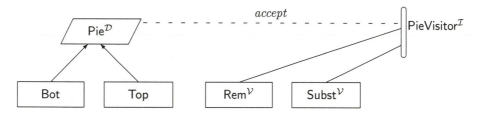

Why is there is a line, not an arrow, from Subst$^\mathcal{V}$ to PieVisitor$^\mathcal{I}$?

57 The Subst$^\mathcal{V}$ visitor **implements** PieVisitor$^\mathcal{I}$, it doesn't *extend* it. Arrows mean "extends," lines mean "implements."

And the dashed line?

58 It tells us the name of the method that connects the datatype to the visitors.

What is the value of
  new Top(new Anchovy(),
    new Top(new Tuna(),
      new Top(new Anchovy(),
        new Top(new Tuna(),
          new Top(new Anchovy(),
            new Bot()))))))
  .*accept*(new LtdSubst$^\mathcal{V}$(2,
                  new Salmon(),
                  new Anchovy())))?

59

Easy:
  new Top(new Salmon(),
    new Top(new Tuna(),
      new Top(new Salmon(),
        new Top(new Tuna(),
          new Top(new Anchovy(),
            new Bot())))))).

Explain what LtdSubst$^\mathcal{V}$ produces.[1]

---
[1] A better name is `LimitedSubstitutionV`, and that is how
we pronounce it.

The methods of LtdSubst$^\mathcal{V}$ replace one fish on
a pie by another as many times as specified
by the first value consumed by LtdSubst$^\mathcal{V}$.

Good. Define LtdSubst$^\mathcal{V}$.

That's easy. We have such a flexible protocol
that we only need to define the essence now.

```
class LtdSubst^V implements PieVisitor^I {
  int c;
  Object n;
  Object o;
  LtdSubst^V(int _c,Object _n,Object _o) {
    c = _c;
    n = _n;
    o = _o; }

  public Pie^D forBot() {
    return new Bot(); }
  public Pie^D forTop(Object t,Pie^D r) {
    if (c == 0)
      return new Top(t,r);
    else
      if (o.equals(t))
        return
          new Top(n,r.accept(this));
      else
        return
          new Top(t,r.accept(this)); }
}
```

What is the value of
  new Top(new Anchovy(),
   new Top(new Tuna(),
    new Top(new Anchovy(),
     new Top(new Tuna(),
      new Top(new Anchovy(),
       new Bot()))))))
  .$accept$(new LtdSubst$^{\mathcal{V}}$(2,
                new Salmon(),
                new Anchovy())))?

62 Oops, there are too few anchovies on this pizza pie:
    new Top(new Salmon(),
     new Top(new Tuna(),
      new Top(new Salmon(),
       new Top(new Tuna(),
        new Top(new Salmon(),
         new Bot())))))).

How come?

63 Because c, the counting field, never changes.

Why doesn't c ever change?

64 Because **this**, the LtdSubst$^{\mathcal{V}}$ that performs the substitutions, never changes.

Can we fix **this**?

65 We can't change **this**, but we can replace **this** with a new LtdSubst$^{\mathcal{V}}$ that reflects the change.

If c stands for the current count, how do we create a LtdSubst$^{\mathcal{V}}$ that shows that we have just substituted one fish by another.

66 Simple, we use
    new LtdSubst$^{\mathcal{V}}$($c-1,n,o$)
  in place of **this**.

The Sixth Bit of Advice

When the additional consumed values change for a self-referential use of a visitor, don't forget to create a new visitor.

Define the new and improved version of LtdSubst$^{\mathcal{V}}$.

67 Voilà.

```
class LtdSubst^V implements PieVisitor^I {
  int c;
  Object n;
  Object o;
  LtdSubst^V(int _c,Object _n,Object _o) {
    c = _c;
    n = _n;
    o = _o; }

  public Pie^D forBot() {
    return new Bot(); }
  public Pie^D forTop(Object t,Pie^D r) {
    if (c == 0)
      return new Top(t,r);
    else
      if (o.equals(t))
        return
          new Top(n,
            r.accept(
              new LtdSubst^V(c − 1,n,o)));
      else
        return
          new Top(t,
            r.accept(
              this)); }
}
```

How does

this

differ from

new LtdSubst$^{\mathcal{V}}(c-1,n,o)$?

68 They are two different LtdSubst$^{\mathcal{V}}$s. One replaces c occurrences of o by n in a pizza pie, and the other one replaces only $c-1$ of them.

How do you feel about protocols now?

69 They are exciting. Let's do more.

7.
Oh My!

Is
  new Flat(**new** Apple(),
   new Flat(**new** Peach(),
    new Bud())))
a flat Tree$^\mathcal{D}$?
	[1] Yes.

Is
  new Flat(**new** Pear(),
   new Bud())
a flat Tree$^\mathcal{D}$?
	[2] Yes, it is also a flat Tree$^\mathcal{D}$.

And how about
  new Split(
  new Bud(),
  new Flat(**new** Fig(),
   new Split(
   new Bud(),
   new Bud()))))?
	[3] No, it is split, so it can't be flat.

Here is one more example:
  new Split(
  new Split(
  new Bud(),
  new Flat(**new** Lemon(),
   new Bud())),
  new Flat(**new** Fig(),
   new Split(
   new Bud(),
   new Bud())))).
Is it flat?
	[4] No, it isn't flat either.

Is the difference between flat trees and split trees obvious now?	[5] Unless there is anything else to Tree$^\mathcal{D}$, it's totally clear.

Good. Then let's move on.	[6] Okay, let's.

Here are some fruits.

```
abstract class Fruit𝒟 {}
```

```
class Peach extends Fruit𝒟 {
  public boolean equals(Object o) {
    return (o instanceof Peach); }
}
```

```
class Apple extends Fruit𝒟 {
  public boolean equals(Object o) {
    return (o instanceof Apple); }
}
```

```
class Pear extends Fruit𝒟 {
  public boolean equals(Object o) {
    return (o instanceof Pear); }
}
```

```
class Lemon extends Fruit𝒟 {
  public boolean equals(Object o) {
    return (o instanceof Lemon); }
}
```

```
class Fig extends Fruit𝒟 {
  public boolean equals(Object o) {
    return (o instanceof Fig); }
}
```

Let's say all Tree𝒟s are either flat, split, or bud. Formulate a rigorous description for Tree𝒟s.

Did you notice that we have redefined the method *equals* in the variants of Fruit𝒟?

Do Tree𝒟's variants contain *equals*?

[7] It does not differ too much from what we have seen before.

```
abstract class Tree𝒟 {}
```

```
class Bud extends Tree𝒟 {}
```

```
class Flat extends Tree𝒟 {
  Fruit𝒟 f;
  Tree𝒟 t;
  Flat(Fruit𝒟 _f,Tree𝒟 _t) {
    f = _f;
    t = _t; }
}
```

```
class Split extends Tree𝒟 {
  Tree𝒟 l;
  Tree𝒟 r;
  Split(Tree𝒟 _l,Tree𝒟 _r) {
    l = _l;
    r = _r; }
}
```

[8] That probably means that we will need to compare fruits and other things.

[9] No, which means we won't compare them, but we could.

How does the datatype $\mathsf{Tree}^{\mathcal{D}}$ differ from all the other datatypes we have seen before?

The name of the new datatype occurs twice in its Split variant.

Let's add a visitor interface whose methods produce **boolean**s.

That just means extending what we have with one method each.

```
interface bTreeVisitor^I {
  boolean forBud();
  boolean forFlat(Fruit^D f,Tree^D t);
  boolean forSplit(Tree^D l,Tree^D r);
}
```

```
class Bud extends Tree^D {
  boolean accept(bTreeVisitor^I ask) {
    return ask.forBud(); }
}
```

Here is the new datatype definition.

```
abstract class Tree^D {
  abstract
    boolean accept(bTreeVisitor^I ask);
}
```

Revise the variants.

```
class Flat extends Tree^D {
  Fruit^D f;
  Tree^D t;
  Flat(Fruit^D _f,Tree^D _t) {
    f = _f;
    t = _t; }

  boolean accept(bTreeVisitor^I ask) {
    return ask.forFlat(f,t); }
}
```

```
class Split extends Tree^D {
  Tree^D l;
  Tree^D r;
  Split(Tree^D _l,Tree^D _r) {
    l = _l;
    r = _r; }

  boolean accept(bTreeVisitor^I ask) {
    return ask.forSplit(l,r); }
}
```

But isn't $\mathsf{bTreeVisitor}^{\mathcal{I}}$ a pretty unusual name?

Yes, it is. Hang in there, we need unusual names for unusual interfaces. Here **b** reminds us that the visitor's methods produce **boolean**s.

12

Okay.

How many methods does the definition of blsFlat$^{\mathcal{V}}$ contain, assuming it implements bTreeVisitor$^{\mathcal{I}}$?

[13] Three, because it works with Tree$^{\mathcal{D}}$s, and the datatype definition for Tree$^{\mathcal{D}}$s has three variants.

What type of values do the methods of blsFlat$^{\mathcal{V}}$ produce?

[14] **boolean**s.

What visitor does blsFlat$^{\mathcal{V}}$ remind us of?

[15] OnlyOnions$^{\mathcal{V}}$.

Here is a skeleton for blsFlat$^{\mathcal{V}}$.

```
class blsFlat^V implements bTreeVisitor^I {
  public
    boolean forBud() {
      return _____ ; }
  public
    boolean forFlat(Fruit^D f,Tree^D t) {
      return _____ ; }
  public
    boolean forSplit(Tree^D l,Tree^D r) {
      return _____ ; }
}
```

Fill in the blanks.

[16] That's easy now.

```
class blsFlat^V implements bTreeVisitor^I {
  public
    boolean forBud() {
      return true; }
  public
    boolean forFlat(Fruit^D f,Tree^D t) {
      return t.accept(this); }
  public
    boolean forSplit(Tree^D l,Tree^D r) {
      return false; }
}
```

Define the blsSplit$^{\mathcal{V}}$ visitor, whose methods check whether a Tree$^{\mathcal{D}}$ is constructed with Split and Bud only.

[17] Here is the easy part.

```
class blsSplit^V implements bTreeVisitor^I {
  public
    boolean forBud() {
      return true; }
  public
    boolean forFlat(Fruit^D f,Tree^D t) {
      return false; }
  public
    boolean forSplit(Tree^D l,Tree^D r) {
      _____ }
}
```

What is difficult about the last line?	[18] We need to check whether both l and r are split trees.

Isn't that easy?	[19] Yes, we just use the methods of blsSplit$^{\mathcal{V}}$ on l and r.

And then?	[20] Then we need to know that both are true.

If $\quad l.accept(\mathbf{this})$ is true, do we need to know whether $\quad r.accept(\mathbf{this})$ is true?	[21] Yes, because if both are true, we have a split tree.

If $\quad l.accept(\mathbf{this})$ is false, do we need to know whether $\quad r.accept(\mathbf{this})$ is true?	[22] No, then the answer is false.

Finish the definition of blsSplit$^{\mathcal{V}}$ using $\quad \mathbf{if}\ (\dots)$ $\qquad \mathbf{return}\ \dots$ $\quad \mathbf{else}$ $\qquad \mathbf{return}\ \dots\ .$	[23] Now we can do it.

```
class blsSplit^V implements bTreeVisitor^I {
  public
    boolean forBud() {
      return true; }
  public
    boolean forFlat(Fruit^D f, Tree^D t) {
      return false; }
  public
    boolean forSplit(Tree^D l, Tree^D r) {
      if¹ (l.accept(this))
        return r.accept(this);
      else
        return false; }
}
```

---

[1] We could have written the **if** ... as
    `return l.accept(this) && r.accept(this)`.

Give an example of a Tree$^\mathcal{D}$ for which the methods of bIsSplit$^\mathcal{V}$ respond with true.

24 There is a trivial one:
new Bud().

How about one with five uses of Split?

25 Here is one:
```
new Split(
  new Split(
    new Bud(),
    new Split(
      new Bud(),
      new Bud())),
  new Split(
    new Bud(),
    new Split(
      new Bud(),
      new Bud()))).
```

Does this Tree$^\mathcal{D}$ have any fruit?

26 No.

Define the bHasFruit$^\mathcal{V}$ visitor.

27 Here it is.

```
class bHasFruit^V
  implements bTreeVisitor^I {
public
  boolean forBud() {
    return false; }
public
  boolean forFlat(Fruit^D f,Tree^D t) {
    return true; }
public
  boolean forSplit(Tree^D l,Tree^D r) {
    if^1 (l.accept(this))
      return true;
    else
      return r.accept(this); }
}
```

---
1 We could have written the **if** ... as
return l.accept(this) || r.accept(this).

What is the height of
  new Split(
   new Split(
    new Bud(),
    new Flat(**new** Lemon(),
     new Bud()))),
   new Flat(**new** Fig(),
    new Split(
     new Bud(),
     new Bud()))))?

[28] 3.

What is the height of
  new Split(
   new Bud(),
   new Flat(**new** Lemon(),
    new Bud())))?

[29] 2.

What is the height of
  new Flat(**new** Lemon(),
   new Bud())?

[30] 1.

What is the height of
  new Bud()?

[31] 0.

So what is the height of a Tree$^{\mathcal{D}}$?

[32] Just as in nature, the height of a tree is the distance from the beginning to the highest bud in the tree.

Do the methods of iHeight$^{\mathcal{V}}$ work on a Tree$^{\mathcal{D}}$?

[33] Yes, and they produce an **int**.

Is that what the i in front of **Height** is all about?

[34] It looks like i stands for **int**, doesn't it?

What is the value of
  new Split(
   new Split(
    new Bud(),
    new Bud()),
   new Flat(**new** Fig(),
    new Flat(**new** Lemon(),
     new Flat(**new** Apple(),
      new Bud())))))
  $.accept($**new** iHeight$^\mathcal{V}$())?

35   4.

Why is the height 4?

36   Because the value of
  new Split(
   new Bud(),
   new Bud())
  $.accept($**new** iHeight$^\mathcal{V}$())

is 1; the value of
  new Flat(**new** Fig(),
   new Flat(**new** Lemon(),
    new Flat(**new** Apple(),
     new Bud())))
  $.accept($**new** iHeight$^\mathcal{V}$())

is 3; and the larger of the two numbers is 3.

And how do we get from 3 to 4?

37   We need to add one to the larger of the numbers so that we don't forget that the original Tree$^\mathcal{D}$ was constructed with Split and those two Tree$^\mathcal{D}$s.

⊔ picks the larger of two numbers, x and y. [1]

---
[1] When you enter this in a file, use
  `Math.max(x,y)`.
`Math` is a class that contains `max` as a (static) method.

38   Oh, that's nice. What kind of methods does iHeight$^\mathcal{V}$ define?

---

iHeight$^\mathcal{V}$'s methods measure the heights of the Tree$^\mathcal{D}$s to which they correspond.

39   Now that's a problem.

| Why? | [40] We defined only **interface**s that produce **boolean**s in this chapter. |

| So what? | [41] The methods of iHeight$^{\mathcal{V}}$ produce **int**s, which are not **boolean**s. |

Okay, so let's define a visitor interface that produces **int**s.

[42] It's almost the same as bTreeVisitor$^{\mathcal{I}}$.

```
interface iTreeVisitor^I {
  int forBud();
  int forFlat(Fruit^D f,Tree^D t);
  int forSplit(Tree^D l,Tree^D r);
}
```

Yes, and once we have that we can add another *accept* method to Tree$^{\mathcal{D}}$.

```
abstract class Tree^D {
  abstract
    boolean accept(bTreeVisitor^I ask);
  abstract
    int accept(iTreeVisitor^I ask);
}
```

[43] Does that mean we can have two methods with the same name in one class?[1]

---
[1] In Java, defining multiple methods with the same name and different input types is called "overloading."

We can have two methods with the same name in the same class as long as the types of the things they consume are distinct.

[44] bTreeVisitor$^{\mathcal{I}}$ is indeed different from iTreeVisitor$^{\mathcal{I}}$, so we can have two versions of *accept* in Tree$^{\mathcal{D}}$.

Add the new *accept* methods to Tree$^{\mathcal{D}}$'s variants. Start with the easy one.

[45] It is easy.

```
class Bud extends Tree^D {
  boolean accept(bTreeVisitor^I ask) {
    return ask.forBud(); }
  int accept(iTreeVisitor^I ask) {
    return ask.forBud(); }
}
```

The others are easy, too. We duplicate *accept*.

46

We must also change the type of what the new *accept* method consumes and produces.

```
class Flat extends Tree𝒟 {
  Fruit𝒟 f;
  Tree𝒟 t;
  Flat(Fruit𝒟 _f,Tree𝒟 _t) {
    f = _f;
    t = _t; }
  ─────────────────────────
  boolean accept(bTreeVisitorℐ ask) {
    return ask.forFlat(f,t); }
  int accept(iTreeVisitorℐ ask) {
    return ask.forFlat(f,t); }
}
```

```
class Split extends Tree𝒟 {
  Tree𝒟 l;
  Tree𝒟 r;
  Split(Tree𝒟 _l,Tree𝒟 _r) {
    l = _l;
    r = _r; }
  ─────────────────────────
  boolean accept(bTreeVisitorℐ ask) {
    return ask.forSplit(l,r); }
  int accept(iTreeVisitorℐ ask) {
    return ask.forSplit(l,r); }
}
```

Here is iHeight𝒱.

47

That's easy now.

```
class iHeight𝒱 implements iTreeVisitorℐ {
  public int forBud() {
    return ─────── ; }
  public int forFlat(Fruit𝒟 f,Tree𝒟 t) {
    return ─────── ; }
  public int forSplit(Tree𝒟 l,Tree𝒟 r) {
    return ─────── ; }
}
```

Complete these methods.

```
class iHeight𝒱 implements iTreeVisitorℐ {
  public int forBud() {
    return 0; }
  public int forFlat(Fruit𝒟 f,Tree𝒟 t) {
    return t.accept(this) + 1; }
  public int forSplit(Tree𝒟 l,Tree𝒟 r) {
    return
      (l.accept(this) ⊔ r.accept(this))
      + 1; }
}
```

What is the value of
  new Split(
    new Bud(),
    new Bud())
  .*accept*(**new** iHeight𝒱())?

1, of course.

And why is it 1?

Because
  new Bud().*accept*(**new** iHeight𝒱())
is 0, the larger of 0 and 0 is 0, and one more is 1.

What is the value of
  new Split(
   new Split(
    new Flat(new Fig(),
     new Bud())),
    new Flat(new Fig(),
     new Bud()))),
   new Flat(new Fig(),
    new Flat(new Lemon(),
     new Flat(new Apple(),
      new Bud())))))
  .accept(
   new tSubst$^\mathcal{V}$(
    new Apple(),
    new Fig())))?

50

If the visitor tSubst$^\mathcal{V}$ substitutes apples for figs, here is what we get:
  new Split(
   new Split(
    new Flat(new Apple(),
     new Bud())),
    new Flat(new Apple(),
     new Bud()))),
   new Flat(new Apple(),
    new Flat(new Lemon(),
     new Flat(new Apple(),
      new Bud())))).

Correct. Define the tSubst$^\mathcal{V}$ visitor.

51

It's like SubstFish$^\mathcal{V}$ and SubstInt$^\mathcal{V}$ from the end of chapter 5, but we can't do it just yet.

What's the problem?

52

Its methods produce Tree$^\mathcal{D}$s, neither **int**s nor **boolean**s, which means that we need to add yet another interface.

```
interface tTreeVisitor^I {
  Tree^D forBud();
  Tree^D forFlat(Fruit^D f, Tree^D t);
  Tree^D forSplit(Tree^D l, Tree^D r);
}
```

Good job. How about the datatype Tree$^\mathcal{D}$.

53

Easy. Here is the abstract one.

```
abstract class Tree^D {
  abstract
    boolean accept(bTreeVisitor^I ask);
  abstract
    int accept(iTreeVisitor^I ask);
  abstract
    Tree^D accept(tTreeVisitor^I ask);
}
```

Oh My!

Define the variants of Tree$^\mathcal{D}$.

No problem.

```
class Bud extends Tree𝒟 {
  boolean accept(bTreeVisitor𝓘 ask) {
    return ask.forBud(); }
  int accept(iTreeVisitor𝓘 ask) {
    return ask.forBud(); }
  Tree𝒟 accept(tTreeVisitor𝓘 ask) {
    return ask.forBud(); }
}
```

```
class Flat extends Tree𝒟 {
  Fruit𝒟 f;
  Tree𝒟 t;
  Flat(Fruit𝒟 _f,Tree𝒟 _t) {
    f = _f;
    t = _t; }

  boolean accept(bTreeVisitor𝓘 ask) {
    return ask.forFlat(f,t); }
  int accept(iTreeVisitor𝓘 ask) {
    return ask.forFlat(f,t); }
  Tree𝒟 accept(tTreeVisitor𝓘 ask) {
    return ask.forFlat(f,t); }
}
```

```
class Split extends Tree𝒟 {
  Tree𝒟 l;
  Tree𝒟 r;
  Split(Tree𝒟 _l,Tree𝒟 _r) {
    l = _l;
    r = _r; }

  boolean accept(bTreeVisitor𝓘 ask) {
    return ask.forSplit(l,r); }
  int accept(iTreeVisitor𝓘 ask) {
    return ask.forSplit(l,r); }
  Tree𝒟 accept(tTreeVisitor𝓘 ask) {
    return ask.forSplit(l,r); }
}
```

Then define tSubst$^\mathcal{V}$.

That's easy, too. It has two fields, one for the new Fruit$^\mathcal{D}$ and one for the old one, and the rest is straightforward.

```
class tSubst^V implements tTreeVisitor^I {
  Fruit^D n;
  Fruit^D o;
  tSubst^V(Fruit^D _n,Fruit^D _o) {
    n = _n;
    o = _o; }

  public Tree^D forBud() {
    return new Bud(); }
  public Tree^D forFlat(Fruit^D f,Tree^D t) {
    if (o.equals(f))
      return new Flat(n,t.accept(this));
    else
      return new Flat(f,t.accept(this)); }
  public Tree^D forSplit(Tree^D l,Tree^D r) {
    return new Split(l.accept(this),
                     r.accept(this)); }
}
```

Here is a Tree$^\mathcal{D}$ that has three Figs:

```
  new Split(
   new Split(
    new Flat(new Fig(),
     new Bud()),
    new Flat(new Fig(),
     new Bud())),
   new Flat(new Fig(),
    new Flat(new Lemon(),
     new Flat(new Apple(),
      new Bud()))))).
```

Now define iOccurs$^\mathcal{V}$, whose methods count how often some Fruit$^\mathcal{D}$ occurs in a tree.

56

Even the visitors are no longer interesting.

```
class iOccurs^V implements iTreeVisitor^I {
  Fruit^D a;
  iOccurs^V(Fruit^D _a) {
    a = _a; }

  public int forBud() {
    return 0; }
  public int forFlat(Fruit^D f,Tree^D t) {
    if (f.equals(a))
      return t.accept(this) + 1;
    else
      return t.accept(this); }
  public int forSplit(Tree^D l,Tree^D r) {
    return
      l.accept(this) + r.accept(this); }
}
```

Do you like your fruit with yogurt?

⁵⁷ We prefer coconut sorbet.

Is it disturbing that we have three nearly identical versions of *accept* in Tree$^\mathcal{D}$s and its variants?

⁵⁸ Copying definitions is always bad. If we make a mistake and copy a definition, we copy mistakes. If we modify one, it's likely that we might forget to modify the other.

Can we avoid it?

⁵⁹ If **boolean** and **int** were classes, we could use Object for **boolean**, **int**, and Tree$^\mathcal{D}$. Unfortunately, they are not.

Remember Integer and Boolean? They make it possible.

⁶⁰ Yes, Boolean is the class that corresponds to **boolean**, and Integer corresponds to **int**.

Here is the **interface** for a protocol that produces Object in place of **boolean**, **int**, and Tree$^\mathcal{D}$.

```
interface TreeVisitor^I {
  Object forBud();
  Object forFlat(Fruit^D f, Tree^D t);
  Object forSplit(Tree^D l, Tree^D r);
}
```

Here is the datatype and the Bud variant.

```
abstract class Tree^D {
  abstract
    Object accept(TreeVisitor^I ask);
}
```

```
class Bud extends Tree^D {
  Object accept(TreeVisitor^I ask) {
    return ask.forBud(); }
}
```

Define the remaining variants of Tree$^\mathcal{D}$.

⁶¹ Here they are.

```
class Flat extends Tree^D {
  Fruit^D f;
  Tree^D t;
  Flat(Fruit^D _f, Tree^D _t) {
    f = _f;
    t = _t; }

  Object accept(TreeVisitor^I ask) {
    return ask.forFlat(f,t); }
}
```

```
class Split extends Tree^D {
  Tree^D l;
  Tree^D r;
  Split(Tree^D _l, Tree^D _r) {
    l = _l;
    r = _r; }

  Object accept(TreeVisitor^I ask) {
    return ask.forSplit(l,r); }
}
```

Good. Now define IsFlat$^\mathcal{V}$, an Object producing version of bIsFlat$^\mathcal{V}$.

That's no big deal.

```
class IsFlat𝒱 implements TreeVisitorℐ {
  public Object forBud() {
    return new Boolean(true); }
  public Object forFlat(Fruit𝒟 f, Tree𝒟 t) {
    return t.accept(this); }
  public Object forSplit(Tree𝒟 l, Tree𝒟 r) {
    return new Boolean(false); }
}
```

And how about IsSplit$^\mathcal{V}$?

Now that's different. Here we need a way to determine the underlying **boolean** of the Boolean that is produced by $l.accept(\mathbf{this})$ in the original definition.

Okay, here it is.

```
class IsSplit𝒱 implements TreeVisitorℐ {
  public Object forBud() {
    return new Boolean(true); }
  public Object forFlat(Fruit𝒟 f, Tree𝒟 t) {
    return new Boolean(false); }
  public Object forSplit(Tree𝒟 l, Tree𝒟 r) {
    if (((Boolean) (l.accept(this)))
        .booleanValue())
      return r.accept(this);
    else
      return new Boolean(false); }
}
```

Oh, because $l.accept(\mathbf{this})$ produces an Object, we must first convert[1] it to a Boolean. Then we can determine the underlying **boolean** with the *booleanValue* method. We have seen this in chapter 5 when we converted an Object to a OneMoreThan.

---

[1] If Java had parametric polymorphism for methods, no downward cast would be necessary for our visitors (Martin Odersky and Philip Wadler, Pizza into Java: Translating Theory into Practice, *Conference Record on Principles of Programming Languages*, 146–159. Paris, 1997).

Will the conversion always work?

Yes, because the Object produced by $l.accept(\mathbf{this})$ is always a Boolean.

The Seventh Bit of Advice

When designing visitor protocols for many different types, create a unifying protocol using Object.

Did you think that was bad? Then study this definition during your next break.

Oh my!

```
class Occurs^V implements TreeVisitor^I {
  Fruit^D a;
  Occurs^V(Fruit^D _a) {
   a = _a; }
  ────────────────────────────
  public Object forBud() {
   return new Integer(0); }
  public Object forFlat(Fruit^D f, Tree^D t) {
   if (f.equals(a))
    return
     new Integer(((Integer)
                 (t.accept(this)))
                .intValue()
                + 1);
   else
    return t.accept(this); }
  public Object forSplit(Tree^D l, Tree^D r) {
   return
    new Integer(((Integer)
                (l.accept(this)))
               .intValue()
               +
               ((Integer)
               (r.accept(this)))
               .intValue()); }
}
```

8.
Like Father, Like Son

What is the value of $(7 + ((4 - 3) \times 5))$?	[1] 12.

What is the value of $(+ \; 7 \; (\times \; (- \; 4 \; 3) \; 5))$?	[2] 12, because we have just rewritten the previous expression with prefix operators.

What is the value of
new Plus(
  new Const(**new** Integer(7)),
  new Prod(
    new Diff(
      new Const(**new** Integer(4)),
      new Const(**new** Integer(3))),
    new Const(**new** Integer(5))))?
	[3] **new** Integer(12),
	
	because we have just rewritten the
	previous expression using Integer and
	constructors.

Where do the constructors come from?	[4] A datatype and its variants that represent arithmetic expressions.

Did you like that?	[5] So far, so good.

What is the value of $(\{7,5\} \cup ((\{4\} \setminus \{3\}) \cap \{5\}))$?	[6] $\{7,5\}$.

What is the value of $(\cup \; \{7,5\} \; (\cap \; (\setminus \; \{4\} \; \{3\}) \; \{5\}))$?	[7] $\{7,5\}$, we just went from infix to prefix notation.

What is the value of $(+ \; \{7,5\} \; (\times \; (- \; \{4\} \; \{3\}) \; \{5\}))$?	[8] $\{7,5\}$, we just renamed the operators.

What is the value of
    new Plus(
        new Const(**new** Empty()
                        .*add*(**new** Integer(7))
                        .*add*(**new** Integer(5))),
        new Prod(
            new Diff(
                new Const(**new** Empty()
                            .*add*(**new** Integer(4))),
                new Const(**new** Empty()
                            .*add*(**new** Integer(3)))),
            new Const(**new** Empty()
                        .*add*(**new** Integer(5))))))?

9 **new** Empty()
    .*add*(**new** Integer(7))
    .*add*(**new** Integer(5)),
        because we have just rewritten the
        previous expression using the constructors.

Where do the constructors come from?

10 A datatype and its variants that represent
set expressions.

Do you still like it?

11 Sure, why not.

Does the arithmetic expression look like the
set expression?

12 Yes, they look the same except for the
constants:
    new Plus(
        new Const($\bullet$),
        new Prod(
            new Diff(
                new Const($\bullet$),
                new Const($\bullet$)),
            new Const($\bullet$))).

Let's say that an expression is either

    a Plus($expr_1, expr_2$),
    a Diff($expr_1, expr_2$),
    a Prod($expr_1, expr_2$), or
    a constant,

where $expr_1$ and $expr_2$ stand for arbitrary
expressions. What should be the visitor
interface?

13 That's a tricky question.

interface ExprVisitor$^\mathcal{I}$ {
  Object *forPlus*(Expr$^\mathcal{D}$ *l*,Expr$^\mathcal{D}$ *r*);
  Object *forDiff*(Expr$^\mathcal{D}$ *l*,Expr$^\mathcal{D}$ *r*);
  Object *forProd*(Expr$^\mathcal{D}$ *l*,Expr$^\mathcal{D}$ *r*);
  Object *forConst*(Object *c*);
}

Good answer. Here is the datatype now.

```
abstract class Expr^D {
  abstract
    Object accept(ExprVisitor^I ask);
}
```

Define the variants of the datatype and equip them with an *accept* method that produces Objects.

```
class Plus extends Expr^D {
  Expr^D l;
  Expr^D r;
  Plus(Expr^D _l,Expr^D _r) {
    l = _l;
    r = _r; }

  Object accept(ExprVisitor^I ask) {
    return ask.forPlus(l,r); }
}
```

```
class Diff extends Expr^D {
  Expr^D l;
  Expr^D r;
  Diff(Expr^D _l,Expr^D _r) {
    l = _l;
    r = _r; }

  Object accept(ExprVisitor^I ask) {
    return ask.forDiff(l,r); }
}
```

```
class Prod extends Expr^D {
  Expr^D l;
  Expr^D r;
  Prod(Expr^D _l,Expr^D _r) {
    l = _l;
    r = _r; }

  Object accept(ExprVisitor^I ask) {
    return ask.forProd(l,r); }
}
```

```
class Const extends Expr^D {
  Object c;
  Const(Object _c) {
    c = _c; }

  Object accept(ExprVisitor^I ask) {
    return ask.forConst(c); }
}
```

Can we now define a visitor whose methods determine the value of an arithmetic expression?

15 Yes, we can. It must have four methods, one per variant, and it is like $\text{Occurs}^{\mathcal{V}}$ from the previous chapter.

How do we add
   new Integer(3)
and
   new Integer(2)?

16 We have done this before. We use the method *intValue* to determine the **int**s that correspond to the Integers, and then add them together.

But what is the result of
   new Integer(3).*intValue*()
   +
   new Integer(2).*intValue*()?

17 An **int**, what else?

How do we turn that into an Integer?

18 We use **new** Integer(...).

Okay, so here is a skeleton of $\text{IntEval}^{\mathcal{V}}$.

```
class IntEval^V implements ExprVisitor^I {
  public Object forPlus(Expr^D l,Expr^D r) {
    return plus(l.accept(this),
                r.accept(this)); }
  public Object forDiff(Expr^D l,Expr^D r) {
    return diff(l.accept(this),
                r.accept(this)); }
  public Object forProd(Expr^D l,Expr^D r) {
    return prod(l.accept(this),
                r.accept(this)); }
  public Object forConst(Object c) {
    return c; }
  Object plus(___1 l,___2 r) {
    return ___3; }
  Object diff(___1 l,___2 r) {
    return ___4; }
  Object prod(___1 l,___2 r) {
    return ___5; }
}
```

19 That's an interesting skeleton. It contains five different kinds of blanks and two of them occur three times each. But we can see the bones only. Where is the beef?

How does *forPlus* work?	[20] It consumes two Expr$^{\mathcal{D}}$s, determines their respective values, and *plus*es them.
How are the values represented?	[21] As Objects, because we are using our most general kind of (and most recent) visitor.

So what kind of values must *plus* consume?	[22] Objects,
	    because that's what
	        l.accept(**this**)
	    and
	        r.accept(**this**)
	    produce.

What must we put in the first and second blanks?	[23] Object.
Can we add Objects?	[24] No, we must convert them to Integers first and extract their underlying **int**s.
Can we convert all Objects to Integers?	[25] No, but all Objects produced by IntEval$^{\mathcal{V}}$ are made with **new** Integer(...), so that this conversion always succeeds.

Is that true? What is the value of
  new Plus(
    new Const(**new** Empty()),
    new Const(**new** Integer(5)))
  .*accept*(**new** IntEval$^{\mathcal{V}}$())?
	[26] Wow. At some level, this is nonsense.

Correct, so sometimes the conversion may fail, because we use an instance of IntEval$^{\mathcal{V}}$ on nonsensical arithmetic expressions.	[27] What should we do?

We agree to avoid such arithmetic expressions.[1]

---

[1] In other words, we have *unsafe* evaluators for our expressions. One way to make them safe is to add a method that checks whether constants are instances of the proper class and that raises an exception [1:chapter 7]. An alternative is to define a visitor that type checks the arithmetic expressions we wish to evaluate.

If we want to add l and r, we write

  new Integer(
    $((Integer)l).intValue()$
    $+$
    $((Integer)r).intValue())$.

Complete the definition now.

And their set expressions, too.

Now it's easy. Here we go.

```
class IntEval^V implements ExprVisitor^I {
  public Object forPlus(Expr^D l,Expr^D r) {
    return plus(l.accept(this),
                r.accept(this)); }
  public Object forDiff(Expr^D l,Expr^D r) {
    return diff(l.accept(this),
                r.accept(this)); }
  public Object forProd(Expr^D l,Expr^D r) {
    return prod(l.accept(this),
                r.accept(this)); }
  public Object forConst(Object c) {
    return c; }
  Object plus(Object l,Object r) {
    return
      new Integer(
        ((Integer)l).intValue()
        +
        ((Integer)r).intValue()); }
  Object diff(Object l,Object r) {
    return
      new Integer(
        ((Integer)l).intValue()
        −
        ((Integer)r).intValue()); }
  Object prod(Object l,Object r) {
    return
      new Integer(
        ((Integer)l).intValue()
        *
        ((Integer)r).intValue()); }
}
```

That one was pretty easy, wasn't it?

30 Yes. Let's implement an ExprVisitor$^{\mathcal{I}}$ for sets.

What do we need to implement one for sets?

31 We certainly need methods for *plus*ing, *diff*ing, and *prod*ing sets.

That's correct, and here is everything.

32 Whoa.

abstract class Set$^{\mathcal{D}}$ {

> Set$^{\mathcal{D}}$ *add*(Integer i) {
>   **if** ($mem(i)$)
>   **return this**;
>   **else**
>   **return new** Add(i,**this**); }

  abstract boolean mem(Integer i);
  abstract Set$^{\mathcal{D}}$ $plus$(Set$^{\mathcal{D}}$ s);
  abstract Set$^{\mathcal{D}}$ $diff$(Set$^{\mathcal{D}}$ s);
  abstract Set$^{\mathcal{D}}$ $prod$(Set$^{\mathcal{D}}$ s);
}

Explain the method in the nested box in your own words.

33 We use our words:

> "As its name says, *add* adds an element to a **set**. If the element is a *mem*ber of the set, the set remains the same; otherwise, a **new** set is constructed with Add."

Why is this so tricky?

34 Constructors always construct, and *add* does not always construct.

Do we need to understand that?

35 Not now, but feel free to absorb it when you have the time.

Define the variants Empty and Add for Set$^{\mathcal{D}}$. [36]   Here we go.

```
class Empty extends Set𝒟 {
  boolean mem(Integer i) {
    return false; }
  Set𝒟 plus(Set𝒟 s) {
    return s; }
  Set𝒟 diff(Set𝒟 s) {
    return new Empty(); }
  Set𝒟 prod(Set𝒟 s) {
    return new Empty(); }
}
```

```
class Add extends Set𝒟 {
  Integer i;
  Set𝒟 s;
  Add(Integer _i,Set𝒟 _s) {
    i = _i;
    s = _s; }
```

```
  boolean mem(Integer n) {
    if (i.equals(n))
      return true;
    else
      return s.mem(n); }
  Set𝒟 plus(Set𝒟 t) {
    return s.plus(t.add(i)); }
  Set𝒟 diff(Set𝒟 t) {
    if (t.mem(i))
      return s.diff(t);
    else
      return s.diff(t).add(i); }
  Set𝒟 prod(Set𝒟 t) {
    if (t.mem(i))
      return s.prod(t).add(i);
    else
      return s.prod(t); }
}
```

Do we need to understand these definitions?	37 Not now, but feel free to think about them when you have the time. We haven't even used visitors to define operations for union, set-difference, and intersection, but we trust you can.

What do we have to change in $\mathsf{IntEval}^{\mathcal{V}}$ to obtain $\mathsf{SetEval}^{\mathcal{V}}$, an evaluator for set expressions?	38 Not much, just *plus*, *diff*, and *prod*.

How should we do that?	39 Oh, that's a piece of pie. We just copy the definition of $\mathsf{IntEval}^{\mathcal{V}}$ and replace its *plus*, *diff*, and *prod* methods.

That's the worst way of doing that.	40 What?

Why should we throw away more than half of what we have?	41 That's true. If we copied the definition and changed it, we would have identical copies of *forPlus*, *forDiff*, *forProd*, and *forConst*. We should reuse this definition.[1]

---

[1] Sometimes we do not have license to see the definitions, so copying might not even be an option.

Yes, and we are about to show you better ways. How do we have to change *plus*, *diff*, and *prod*?

42 That part is easy:

```
Object plus(Object l,Object r) {
  return ((SetᴰlÁ)l).plus((Setᴰ)r); }
```
and
```
Object diff(Object l,Object r) {
  return ((Setᴰ)l).diff((Setᴰ)r); }
```
and
```
Object prod(Object l,Object r) {
  return ((Setᴰ)l).prod((Setᴰ)r); }.
```

Very good, and if we define SetEval$^\mathcal{V}$ as an extension of IntEval$^\mathcal{V}$, that's all we have to put inside of SetEval$^\mathcal{V}$.

```
class SetEvalᵛ extends IntEvalᵛ {
  Object plus(Object l,Object r) {
    return ((Setᴰ)l).plus((Setᴰ)r); }
  Object diff(Object l,Object r) {
    return ((Setᴰ)l).diff((Setᴰ)r); }
  Object prod(Object l,Object r) {
    return ((Setᴰ)l).prod((Setᴰ)r); }
}
```

[43] Now that's much easier than copying and modifying.

Is it like *equals*?

[44] Yes, when we include *equals* in our class definitions, we override the one in Object. Here, we override the methods *plus*, *diff*, and *prod* as we extend IntEval$^\mathcal{V}$.

How many methods from IntEval$^\mathcal{V}$ are overridden in SetEval$^\mathcal{V}$?

[45] Three.

How many methods from IntEval$^\mathcal{V}$ are not overridden in SetEval$^\mathcal{V}$?

[46] Four: *forPlus*, *forDiff*, *forProd*, and *forConst*.

Does SetEval$^\mathcal{V}$ implement ExprVisitor$^\mathcal{I}$?

[47] It doesn't say so.

Does SetEval$^\mathcal{V}$ extend IntEval$^\mathcal{V}$?

[48] It says so.

Does IntEval$^\mathcal{V}$ implement ExprVisitor$^\mathcal{I}$?

[49] It says so.

Does SetEval$^\mathcal{V}$ implement ExprVisitor$^\mathcal{I}$?

[50] By implication.

That's correct. What is the value of
   new Prod(
     new Const(**new** Empty()
          .*add*(**new** Integer(7))),
     new Const(**new** Empty()
          .*add*(**new** Integer(3))))
   .*accept*(**new** SetEval$^{\mathcal{V}}$())?

51   Interesting question. How does this work now?

What type of value is
   new Prod(
     new Const(**new** Empty()
          .*add*(**new** Integer(7))),
     new Const(**new** Empty()
          .*add*(**new** Integer(3))))?

52   It is a Prod and therefore an Expr$^{\mathcal{D}}$.

And what does *accept* consume?

53   An instance of SetEval$^{\mathcal{V}}$, but its type is ExprVisitor$^{\mathcal{I}}$.

What is
   new SetEval$^{\mathcal{V}}$().*forProd*(
     new Const(**new** Empty()
          .*add*(**new** Integer(7))),
     new Const(**new** Empty()
          .*add*(**new** Integer(3))))?

54   That's what we need to determine the value of next, because it is

$$ask.forProd(l,r),$$

with *ask*, *l*, and *r* replaced by what they stand for.

Where is the definition of SetEval$^{\mathcal{V}}$'s method *forProd*?

55   It is in IntEval$^{\mathcal{V}}$.

Suppose we had the values of
   new Const(**new** Empty()
          .*add*(**new** Integer(7)))
   .*accept*(**this**)
and
   new Const(**new** Empty()
          .*add*(**new** Integer(3)))
   .*accept*(**this**).
What would we have to evaluate next?

56   If their values were A and B, we would have to determine the value of

$$prod(A,B).$$

Isn't that strange?	**57** Why?

So far, we have always used a method on a particular object.

58 That's true. What is the object with which we use $prod(A,B)$?

It is **this** object.

59 Oh, does that mean we should evaluate

new SetEval$^\mathcal{V}$().$prod(A,B)$?

Absolutely. If the use of a method omits the object, we take the one that we were working with before.

60 That clarifies things.

Good. And now what?

61 Now we still need to determine the values of
new Const(**new** Empty()
                    .add(**new** Integer(7)))
  .$accept$(**this**)

and

new Const(**new** Empty()
                    .add(**new** Integer(3)))
  .$accept$(**this**).

The values are obviously
  new Empty()
  .add(**new** Integer(7))
and
  new Empty()
  .add(**new** Integer(3)).

Where is the definition of *forConst* that determines these values?

62 It, too, is in IntEval$^\mathcal{V}$.

Here is the next expression in our sequence:
  new SetEval$^\mathcal{V}$()
  .$prod$(**new** Empty()
        .add(**new** Integer(7)),
        new Empty()
        .add(**new** Integer(3))).

Where does *prod* come from?

63 The object is an instance of SetEval$^\mathcal{V}$, which overrides the *prod* method in IntEval$^\mathcal{V}$ with its own.

What next?	[64] Next we need to determine the value of $$((Set^{\mathcal{D}})(\textbf{new } Empty()$$ $$.add(\textbf{new } Integer(7))))$$ $$.prod((Set^{\mathcal{D}})\textbf{new } Empty()$$ $$.add(\textbf{new } Integer(3)))),$$ because it is $$((Set^{\mathcal{D}})(l.accept(\textbf{this})))$$ $$.prod((Set^{\mathcal{D}})r.accept(\textbf{this}))$$ with $l.accept(\textbf{this})$ and $r.accept(\textbf{this})$ replaced by their respective values.
Is $$\textbf{new } Empty().add(\textbf{new } Integer(7))$$ an instance of $Set^{\mathcal{D}}$?	[65] Of course it is, but the type of $l.accept(\textbf{this})$, which is where it comes from, is Object.
And how about $$\textbf{new } Empty().add(\textbf{new } Integer(3))?$$	[66] It's the same.
And that is why the method must contain a conversion from Object to $Set^{\mathcal{D}}$s.	[67] This example makes the need for conversions obvious again.
Time for the last question. Where does this *prod* come from now?	[68] This one belongs to $Set^{\mathcal{D}}$ or more precisely its Empty and Add variants.
And what does *prod* do?	[69] It determines the intersection of one $Set^{\mathcal{D}}$ with another $Set^{\mathcal{D}}$, but didn't we agree that the previous question was the last question on that topic?
We overrode that, too.	[70] Thanks, guys.
Is it natural that $SetEval^{\mathcal{V}}$ extends $IntEval^{\mathcal{V}}$?	[71] No, not at all.

Why did we do that?

72

Because we defined IntEval$^{\mathcal{V}}$ first.[1]

---

[1] Sometimes we may need to extend classes that are used in several different programs. Unless we wish to maintain multiple copies of the same class, we should extend it.—Java is object-oriented, so it may also be the case that we acquire the object code of a class and its interface, but not its source text. If we wish to enrich the functionality of this kind of class, we must also extend it.

But just because something works, it doesn't mean it's rational.

73

Yes, let's do better. We have defined all these classes ourselves, so we are free to rearrange them any way we want.

What distinguishes IntEval$^{\mathcal{V}}$ from SetEval$^{\mathcal{V}}$?

74

The methods *plus*, *diff*, and *prod*.

What are the pieces that they have in common?

75

They share the methods *forPlus*, *forDiff*, *forProd*, and *forConst*.

Good. Here is how we express that.

76

Isn't this abstract class like Point$^{\mathcal{D}}$?

```
abstract class Eval^D
  implements ExprVisitor^I {
  public Object forPlus(Expr^D l,Expr^D r) {
    return plus(l.accept(this),
                r.accept(this)); }
  public Object forDiff(Expr^D l,Expr^D r) {
    return diff(l.accept(this),
                r.accept(this)); }
  public Object forProd(Expr^D l,Expr^D r) {
    return prod(l.accept(this),
                r.accept(this)); }
  public Object forConst(Object c) {
    return c; }
  abstract
    Object plus(Object l,Object r);
  abstract
    Object diff(Object l,Object r);
  abstract
    Object prod(Object l,Object r);
}
```

Yes, we can think of it as a datatype for $\mathsf{Eval}^{\mathcal{D}}$ visitors that collects all the common elements as concrete methods. The pieces that differ from one variant to another are specified as abstract methods.

77 What do we do now?

We define $\mathsf{IntEval}^{\mathcal{V}}$ extending $\mathsf{Eval}^{\mathcal{D}}$.

```
class IntEvalᵛ extends Evalᴰ {
  Object plus(Object l,Object r) {
   return
    new Integer(
     ((Integer)l).intValue()
     +
     ((Integer)r).intValue()); }
  Object diff(Object l,Object r) {
   return
    new Integer(
     ((Integer)l).intValue()

     −
     ((Integer)r).intValue()); }
  Object prod(Object l,Object r) {
   return
    new Integer(
     ((Integer)l).intValue()

     ∗
     ((Integer)r).intValue()); }
}
```

Define $\mathsf{SetEval}^{\mathcal{V}}$.

78 It is basically like the original but extends $\mathsf{Eval}^{\mathcal{D}}$, not $\mathsf{IntEval}^{\mathcal{V}}$.

```
class SetEvalᵛ extends Evalᴰ {
  Object plus(Object l,Object r) {
   return ((Setᴰ)l).plus((Setᴰ)r); }
  Object diff(Object l,Object r) {
   return ((Setᴰ)l).diff((Setᴰ)r); }
  Object prod(Object l,Object r) {
   return ((Setᴰ)l).prod((Setᴰ)r); }
}
```

Is it natural for two evaluators to be on the same footing?

79 Much more so than one extending the other.

Time for supper.

80 If you are neither hungry nor tired, you may continue.

Remember Subst$^\mathcal{V}$ from chapter 6?

Yes, and LtdSubst$^\mathcal{V}$, too.

```
class Subst^V implements PieVisitor^I {
  Object n;
  Object o;
  Subst^V(Object _n,Object _o) {
    n = _n;
    o = _o; }
  ─────────────────────────────
  public Pie^D forBot() {
    return new Bot(); }
  public Pie^D forTop(Object t,Pie^D r) {
    if (o.equals(t))
      return
        new Top(n,r.accept(this));
    else
      return
        new Top(t,r.accept(this)); }
}
```

```
class LtdSubst^V implements PieVisitor^I {
  int c;
  Object n;
  Object o;
  LtdSubst^V(int _c,Object _n,Object _o) {
    c = _c;
    n = _n;
    o = _o; }
  ─────────────────────────────
  public Pie^D forBot() {
    return new Bot(); }
  public Pie^D forTop(Object t,Pie^D r) {
    if (c == 0)
      return new Top(t,r);
    else
      if (o.equals(t))
        return
          new Top (n,
            r.accept(
              new LtdSubst^V(c − 1,n,o)));
      else
        return
          new Top(t,r.accept(this)); }
}
```

What do the two visitors have in common?

Many things: n, o, and *forBot*.

Where do they differ?

They differ in *forTop*, but LtdSubst$^\mathcal{V}$ also has an extra field.

And where do we put the pieces that two classes have in common?

We put them into an abstract class.

What else does the abstract class contain?

It specifies the pieces that are different if they are needed for all extensions.

Define the **abstract class** $Subst^{\mathcal{D}}$, which contains all the common pieces and specifies what a concrete pie substituter must contain in addition.

It's not a big deal, except for the fields.

```
abstract class Subst^D
  implements PieVisitor^I {
  Object n;
  Object o;
  public Pie^D forBot() {
   return new Bot(); }
  public
   abstract Pie^D forTop(Object t,Pie^D r);
}
```

We can define $Subst^{\mathcal{V}}$ by extending $Subst^{\mathcal{D}}$.

It also extends $Subst^{\mathcal{D}}$.

```
class Subst^V extends Subst^D {
 Subst^V(Object _n,Object _o) {
  n = _n;
  o = _o; }

 public Pie^D forTop(Object t,Pie^D r) {
  if (o.equals(t))
   return
    new Top(n,r.accept(this));
  else
   return
    new Top(t,r.accept(this)); }
}
```

```
class LtdSubst^V extends Subst^D {
  int c;
  LtdSubst^V(int _c,Object _n,Object _o) {
   n = _n;
   o = _o;
   c = _c; }

  public Pie^D forTop(Object t,Pie^D r) {
   if (c == 0)
    return new Top(t,r);
   else
    if (o.equals(t))
     return
      new Top(n,
       r.accept(
        new LtdSubst^V(c - 1,n,o)));
    else
     return
      new Top(t,r.accept(this)); }
}
```

Define $LtdSubst^{\mathcal{V}}$.

Do the two remaining classes still have things in common?

No, but the constructors have some overlap. Shouldn't we lift the $Subst^{\mathcal{V}}$ constructor into $Subst^{\mathcal{D}}$, because it holds the common elements?

That's a great idea. Here is the new version of Subst$^\mathcal{D}$.

```
abstract class Subst^D
  implements PieVisitor^I {
Object n;
Object o;
Subst^D(Object _n,Object _o) {
  n = _n;
  o = _o; }

public Pie^D forBot() {
  return new Bot(); }
public
  abstract Pie^D forTop(Object t,Pie^D r);
}
```

Revise Subst$^\mathcal{V}$ and LtdSubst$^\mathcal{V}$.

We must use **super** in the constructors.

```
class Subst^V extends Subst^D {
  Subst^V(Object _n,Object _o) {
    super(_n,_o); }

  public Pie^D forTop(Object t,Pie^D r) {
    if (o.equals(t))
      return
        new Top(n,r.accept(this));
    else
      return
        new Top(t,r.accept(this)); }
}
```

```
class LtdSubst^V extends Subst^D {
  int c;
  LtdSubst^V(int _c,Object _n,Object _o) {
    super(_n,_o);
    c = _c; }

  public Pie^D forTop(Object t,Pie^D r) {
    if (c == 0)
      return new Top(t,r);
    else
      if (o.equals(t))
        return
          new Top(n,
            r.accept(
              new LtdSubst^V(c-1,n,o)));
      else
        return
          new Top(t,r.accept(this)); }
}
```

Was that first part easy?

As pie.

Chapter 8

That's neat. How about some art work?

91 Is this called a pie chart?

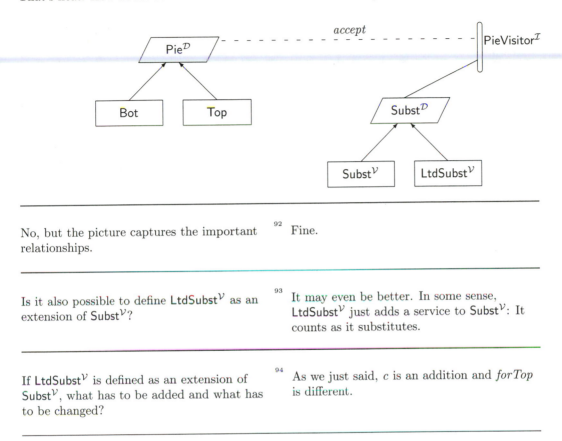

No, but the picture captures the important relationships.

92 Fine.

Is it also possible to define LtdSubst$^{\mathcal{V}}$ as an extension of Subst$^{\mathcal{V}}$?

93 It may even be better. In some sense, LtdSubst$^{\mathcal{V}}$ just adds a service to Subst$^{\mathcal{V}}$: It counts as it substitutes.

If LtdSubst$^{\mathcal{V}}$ is defined as an extension of Subst$^{\mathcal{V}}$, what has to be added and what has to be changed?

94 As we just said, c is an addition and *forTop* is different.

The Eighth Bit of Advice

When extending a class, use overriding to enrich its functionality.

Here is the good old definition of $\mathsf{Subst}^{\mathcal{V}}$ from chapter 6 one more time.

```
class SubstV implements PieVisitorI {
  Object n;
  Object o;
  SubstV(Object _n,Object _o) {
    n = _n;
    o = _o; }

  public PieD forBot() {
    return new Bot(); }
  public PieD forTop(Object t,PieD r) {
    if (o.equals(t))
      return
        new Top(n,r.accept(this));
    else
      return
        new Top(t,r.accept(this)); }
}
```

Define $\mathsf{LtdSubst}^{\mathcal{V}}$ as an extension of $\mathsf{Subst}^{\mathcal{V}}$.

The rest follows naturally, just as with the evaluators and the previous version of these two classes.

```
class LtdSubstV extends SubstV {
  int c;
  LtdSubstV(int _c,Object _n,Object _o) {
    super(_n,_o);
    c = _c; }

  public PieD forTop(Object t,PieD r) {
    if (c == 0)
      return new Top(t,r);
    else
      if (o.equals(t))
        return
          new Top(n,
            r.accept(
              new LtdSubstV(c − 1,n,o)));
      else
        return
          new Top(t,r.accept(this)); }
}
```

Let's draw a picture.

Fine, and don't forget to use lines, rather than arrows, for **implements**.

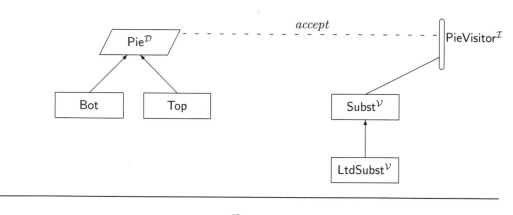

You deserve a super-deluxe pizza now.

It's already on its way.

Chapter 8

9.
Be a Good Visitor

Remember Point$^{\mathcal{D}}$? If not, here is the
datatype with one additional method, *minus*.
We will talk about *minus* when we need it,
but for now, just recall Point$^{\mathcal{D}}$'s variants.

```
abstract class Point^D {
  int x;
  int y;
  Point^D(int _x,int _y) {
    x = _x;
    y = _y; }
  ─────────────────────────────
  boolean closerToO(Point^D p) {
    return
      distanceToO() ≤ p.distanceToO(); }
  Point^D minus(Point^D p) {
    return
      new CartesianPt(x − p.x,y − p.y); }
  abstract int distanceToO();
}
```

Good. Take a look at this extension of
ManhattanPt.

```
class ShadowedManhattanPt
  extends ManhattanPt {
  int Δ_x;
  int Δ_y;
  ShadowedManhattanPt(int _x,
                      int _y,
                      int _Δ_x,
                      int _Δ_y) {
    super(_x,_y);
    Δ_x = _Δ_x;
    Δ_y = _Δ_y; }
  ─────────────────────────────
  int distanceToO() {
    return
      super.distanceToO() + Δ_x + Δ_y; }
}
```

What is unusual about the constructor?

1

It has been a long time since we discussed
the datatype Point$^{\mathcal{D}}$ and its variants, but
they are not that easy to forget.

```
class CartesianPt extends Point^D {
  CartesianPt(int _x,int _y) {
    super(_x,_y); }
  ─────────────────────────────
  int distanceToO() {
    return ⌊√(x² + y²)⌋; }
}
```

```
class ManhattanPt extends Point^D {
  ManhattanPt(int _x,int _y) {
    super(_x,_y); }
  ─────────────────────────────
  int distanceToO() {
    return x + y; }
}
```

2

It uses
$$\Delta_x = {}_-\Delta_x;$$
$$\Delta_y = {}_-\Delta_y;$$
in addition to **super**(_x,_y).

And what does that mean?	[3] By using **super** on the first two values consumed, the constructor creates a ShadowedManhattanPt with proper x and y fields. The rest guarantees that this newly created point also contains values for the two additional fields.

Okay. So what is a ShadowedManhattanPt?	[4] It is a ManhattanPt with two additional fields: Δ_x and Δ_y. These two represent the information that determines how far the shadow is from the point with the fields x and y.

Is this a ShadowedManhattanPt: **new** ShadowedManhattanPt(2,3,1,0)?	[5] Yes.

What is unusual about *distanceToO*?	[6] Unlike any other method we have seen before, it contains the word **super**. So far, we have only seen it used in constructors. What does it mean?

Here, **super**.*distanceToO* refers to the method definition of *distanceToO* that is relevant in the class that ShadowedManhattanPt extends.	[7] Okay. That means we just add x and y when we evaluate **super**.*distanceToO*().

Correct. But what would we have done if ManhattanPt had not defined *distanceToO*?	[8] Then we would refer to the definition in the class that ManhattanPt extends, right?

Yes, and so on. What is the value of **new** ShadowedManhattanPt(2,3,1,0) .*distanceToO*()?	[9] It is 6, because $2 + 3$ is 5, and then we have to add 1 and 0.

Precisely. Now take a look at this extension of CartesianPt.

```
class ShadowedCartesianPt
  extends CartesianPt {
  int Δ_x;
  int Δ_y;
  ShadowedCartesianPt(int _x,
                      int _y,
                      int _Δ_x,
                      int _Δ_y) {
    super(_x,_y);
    Δ_x = _Δ_x;
    Δ_y = _Δ_y; }
```
```
  int distanceToO() {
    return
      super.distanceToO()
      +
      ⌊√(Δ_x² + Δ_y²)⌋; }
}
```

What is unusual about the constructor?

10 Nothing. We just discussed this kind of constructor for ShadowedManhattanPt.

Is this a ShadowedCartesianPt:
new ShadowedCartesianPt(12,5,3,4)?

11 Yes.

And what is the value of
new ShadowedCartesianPt(12,5,3,4)
.distanceToO()?

12 It is 18, because the distance of the Cartesian point (12,5) is 13, and then we add 5, because that is the value of

$$\sqrt{\Delta_x^2 + \Delta_y^2}$$

with Δ_x replaced by 3 and Δ_y replaced by 4.

What do we expect?

13 17, obviously.

Why 17?	[14] Because we need to think of this point as if it were $\qquad$ **new** CartesianPt(15,9).

We need to add Δ_x to x and Δ_y to y when we think of a ShadowedCartesianPt.	[15] And indeed, the value of $\qquad$ **new** CartesianPt(15,9) $\qquad$.$distanceToO()$ is 17.

Does this explain how $distanceToO$ should measure the distance of a ShadowedCartesianPt to the origin?	[16] Completely. It should make a new CartesianPt by adding the corresponding fields and should then measure the distance of that new point to the origin.

Revise the definition of ShadowedCartesianPt accordingly.	[17] Okay.

```
class ShadowedCartesianPt
    extends CartesianPt {
  int Δ_x;
  int Δ_y;
  ShadowedCartesianPt(int _x,
                      int _y,
                      int _Δ_x,
                      int _Δ_y) {
    super(_x,_y);
    Δ_x = _Δ_x;
    Δ_y = _Δ_y; }

  int distanceToO() {
    return
      new CartesianPt(x + Δ_x,y + Δ_y)
      .distanceToO(); }
}
```

Do we still need the new CartesianPt after $distanceToO$ has determined the distance?	[18] No, once we have the distance, we have no need for this point.[1]

---

[1] And neither does Java. Object-oriented languages manage memory so that programmers can focus on the difficult parts of design and implementation.

Correct. What is the value of
  new CartesianPt(3,4)
  .closerToO(
    new ShadowedCartesianPt(1,5,1,2))?

[19] true,
  because the distance of the CartesianPt to
  the origin is 5, while that of the
  ShadowedCartesianPt is 7.

How did we determine that value?

[20] That's obvious.

Is the rest of this chapter obvious, too?

[21] What?

That was a hint that now is a good time to
take a break.

[22] Oh. Well, that makes the hint obvious.

Come back fully rested. You will more than
need it.

[23] Fine.

Are sandwiches square meals for you?

[24] They can be well-rounded.

Here are circles and squares.

```
class Circle extends Shape^D {
  int r;
  Circle(int _r) {
    r = _r; }

  boolean accept(ShapeVisitor^I ask) {
    return ask.forCircle(r); }
}
```

```
class Square extends Shape^D {
  int s;
  Square(int _s) {
    s = _s; }

  boolean accept(ShapeVisitor^I ask) {
    return ask.forSquare(s); }
}
```

[25] Then this must be the datatype that goes
with it.

```
abstract class Shape^D {
  abstract
    boolean accept(ShapeVisitor^I ask);
}
```

Very good. We also need an interface, and here it is.

> **interface** ShapeVisitor$^\mathcal{I}$ {
>   **boolean** *forCircle*(**int** *r*);
>   **boolean** *forSquare*(**int** *s*);
>   **boolean** *forTrans*(Point$^\mathcal{D}$ *q*,Shape$^\mathcal{D}$ *s*);
> }

26 It suggests that there is another variant: Trans.

Yes and we will need this third variant.

> **class** Trans[1] **extends** Shape$^\mathcal{D}$ {
>   Point$^\mathcal{D}$ *q*;
>   Shape$^\mathcal{D}$ *s*;
>   Trans(Point$^\mathcal{D}$ _*q*,Shape$^\mathcal{D}$ _*s*) {
>   *q* = _*q*;
>   *s* = _*s*; }
>
> _____
>
>   **boolean** *accept*(ShapeVisitor$^\mathcal{I}$ *ask*) {
>   **return** *ask.forTrans*(*q*,*s*); }
> }

27 Okay, now this looks pretty straightforward, but what's the point?

---

[1] A better name is `Translation`.

Let's create a circle.

28 No problem:

$$\textbf{new } \mathsf{Circle}(10).$$

How should we think about that circle?

29 We should think about it as a circle with radius 10.

Good. So how should we think about
  new Square(10)?

30 Well, that's a square whose sides are 10 units long.

Where are our circle and square located?

31 What does that mean?

Suppose we wish to determine whether some CartesianPt is inside of the circle?

[32] In that case, we must think of the circle as being drawn around the origin.

And how about the square?

[33] There are many ways to think about the location of the square.

Pick one.

[34] Let's say the square's southwest corner sits on the origin.

That will do. Is the CartesianPt with x coordinate 10 and y coordinate 10 inside the square?

[35] Yes, it is. but barely.

And how about the circle?

[36] Certainly not, because the circle's radius is 10, but the distance of the point to the origin is 14.

Are all circles and squares located at the origin?

[37] We have no choice so far, because Circle and Square only contain one field each: the radius and the length of a side, respectively.

This is where Trans comes in. What is
  new Trans(
    new CartesianPt(5,6),
    new Circle(10))?

[38] Aha. With Trans we can place a circle of radius 10 at a point like
    new CartesianPt(5,6).

How do we place a square's southwest corner at new CartesianPt(5,6)?

[39] Also with Trans:
  new Trans(
    new CartesianPt(5,6),
    new Square(10)).

Is new CartesianPt(10,10) inside either the circle or the square that we just referred to?

[40] It is inside both of them.

How do we determine whether some point is inside a circle?	[41] If the circle is located at the origin, it is simple. We determine the distance of the point to the origin and whether it is smaller than the radius.
How do we determine whether some point is inside a square?	[42] If the square is located at the origin, it is simple. We check whether the point's x coordinate is between 0 and s, the length of the side of the square.
Is that all?	[43] No, we also need to do that for the y coordinate.
Aren't we on a roll?	[44] We have only done the easy stuff so far. It is not clear how to check these things when the circle or the square are not located at the origin.
Let's take a look at our circle around **new** CartesianPt(5,6) again. Can we think of this point as the origin?	[45] We can if we translate all other points by an appropriate amount.
By how much?	[46] By 5 in the x direction and 6 in the y direction, respectively.
How could we translate the points by an appropriate amount?	[47] We could subtract the appropriate amount from each point.
Is there a method in Point$^{\mathcal{D}}$ that accomplishes that?	[48] Yes. Is that why we included *minus* in the new definition of Point$^{\mathcal{D}}$?

Indeed. And now we can define the visitor HasPt$^\mathcal{V}$, whose methods determine whether some Shape$^\mathcal{D}$ has a Point$^\mathcal{D}$ inside of it.

```
class HasPtᵛ implements ShapeVisitorᴵ {
  Pointᴰ p;
  HasPtᵛ(Pointᴰ _p) {
    p = _p; }

  public boolean forCircle(int r) {
    return p.distanceToO() ≤ r; }
  public boolean forSquare(int s) {
    if¹ (p.x ≤ s)
      return (p.y ≤ s);
    else
      return false; }
  public
    boolean forTrans(Pointᴰ q,Shapeᴰ s) {
      return s.accept(
               new HasPtᵛ(p.minus(q))); }
}
```

[49] The three methods put into algebra what we just discussed.

---

¹ We could have written the **if** ... as
return (p.x <= s) && (p.y <= s).

What is the value of
  new Circle(10)
  .accept(
  new HasPt$^\mathcal{V}$(new CartesianPt(10,10)))?

[50] We said that this point wasn't inside of that circle, so the answer is false.

Good. And what is the value of
  new Square(10)
  .accept(
  new HasPt$^\mathcal{V}$(new CartesianPt(10,10)))?

[51] true.

Let's consider something a bit more interesting. What is the value of
  new Trans(
  new CartesianPt(5,6),
  new Circle(10))
  .accept(
  new HasPt$^\mathcal{V}$(new CartesianPt(10,10)))?

[52] We already considered that one, too. The value is true, because the circle's origin is at new CartesianPt(5,6).

Right. And how about this:
new Trans(
  new CartesianPt(5,4),
  new Trans(
   new CartesianPt(5,6),
   new Circle(10)))
 .*accept*(
  new HasPt$^\mathcal{V}$(**new** CartesianPt(10,10)))?

[53] Now that is tricky. We used Trans twice, which we should have expected given Trans's definition.

But what is the value?

[54] First, we have to find out whether
    new Trans(
     new CartesianPt(5,6),
     new Circle(10))
    .*accept*(
     new HasPt$^\mathcal{V}$(**new** CartesianPt(5,6)))
    is true or false.

And then?

[55] Second, we need to look at
    new Circle(10)
    .*accept*(
     new HasPt$^\mathcal{V}$(**new** CartesianPt(0,0))),
    but the value of this is obviously true.

Very good. Can we nest Trans three times?

[56] Ten times, if we wish, because a Trans contains a Shape$^\mathcal{D}$, and that allows us to nest things as often as needed.

Ready to begin?

[57] What? Wasn't that it?

No. The exciting part is about to start.

[58] We are all eyes.

How can we project a cube of cheese to a piece of paper?

[59] It becomes a square, obviously.

And the orange on top?

[60] A circle, Transed appropriately.

Can we think of the two objects as one?

61 We can, but we have no way of saying that a circle and a square belong together.

Here is our way.

```
class Union extends Shape^D {
  Shape^D s;
  Shape^D t;
  Union(Shape^D _s,Shape^D _t) {
    s = _s;
    t = _t; }

  boolean accept(ShapeVisitor^I ask) {
    return _____; }
}
```

62 That looks obvious after the fact. But why is there a blank in *accept*?

What do we know from Circle, Square, and Trans about *accept*?

63 We know that a ShapeVisitor^I contains one method each for the Circle, Square, and Trans variants. And each of these methods consumes the fields of the respective kinds of objects.

So what should we do now?

64 We need to change ShapeVisitor^I so that it specifies a method for the Union variant in addition to the methods for the existing variants.

Correct, except that we won't allow ourselves to change ShapeVisitor^I.

65 Why can't we change it?

Just to make the problem more interesting.

66 In that case, we're stuck.

We would be stuck, but fortunately we can extend **interface**s. Take a look at this.

```
interface UnionVisitor^I
  extends ShapeVisitor^I {
  boolean forUnion(Shape^D s,Shape^D t);
}
```

Basically.[1] This extension produces an interface that contains all the obligations (*i.e.*, names of methods and what they consume and produce) of ShapeVisitor^I and the additional one named *forUnion*.

---
[1] Unlike a class, an interface can actually extend several other interfaces. A class can implement several different interfaces.

Yes it should, but because UnionVisitor^I extends ShapeVisitor^I, it is also a ShapeVisitor^I.

Perfect reasoning. Here is the completed definition of Union.

```
class Union extends Shape^D {
  Shape^D s;
  Shape^D t;
  Union(Shape^D _s,Shape^D _t) {
    s = _s;
    t = _t; }

  boolean accept(ShapeVisitor^I ask) {
    return
      ((UnionVisitor^I)ask).forUnion(s,t); }
}
```

67 Which means that we extend **interface**s the way we extend **class**es.

68 Does that mean *accept* in Union should receive a UnionVisitor^I, so that it can use the *forUnion* method?

69 We have been here before. Our *accept* method must consume a ShapeVisitor^I and fortunately every UnionVisitor^I implements a ShapeVisitor^I, too. But if we know that *accept* consumes a UnionVisitor^I, we can convert the ShapeVisitor^I to a UnionVisitor^I and invoke the *forUnion* method.

70 And it makes complete sense.

Let's create a Union shape.

71
That's trivial.

```
new Trans(
  new CartesianPt(12,2),
  new Union(
    new Square(10),
    new Trans(
      new CartesianPt(4,4),
      new Circle(5)))).
```

That's an interesting shape. Should we check whether

new CartesianPt(12,16)

is inside?

We can't. HasPt$^{\mathcal{V}}$ is only a ShapeVisitor$^{\mathcal{I}}$, it is not a UnionVisitor$^{\mathcal{I}}$.

Could it be a UnionVisitor$^{\mathcal{I}}$?

No. It does not provide the method *forUnion*.

Define UnionHasPt$^{\mathcal{V}}$, which extends HasPt$^{\mathcal{V}}$ with an appropriate method *forUnion*.

Here it is. Its method checks whether the point is in one or the other part of a union. The other methods come from HasPt$^{\mathcal{V}}$.

```
class UnionHasPtᵛ extends HasPtᵛ {
  UnionHasPtᵛ(Pointᴰ _p) {
    super(_p); }

  boolean forUnion(Shapeᴰ s,Shapeᴰ t) {
    if¹ (s.accept(this))
      return true;
    else
      return t.accept(this); }
}
```

[1] We could have written the **if** . . . as
`return s.accept(this) || t.accept(this).`

Does UnionHasPt$^{\mathcal{V}}$ contain *forUnion*?

Of course, we just put it in.

Is UnionHasPt$^\mathcal{V}$ a UnionVisitor$^\mathcal{I}$?

Correct, but unfortunately we have to add three more words to make this explicit.

```
class UnionHasPtᵛ
  extends HasPtᵛ
  implements UnionVisitorᴵ {
UnionHasPtᵛ(Pointᴰ _p) {
  super(_p); }
```
―――――――――――――――――
```
public
  boolean forUnion(Shapeᴰ s,Shapeᴰ t) {
  if (s.accept(this))
    return true;
  else
    return t.accept(this); }
}
```

Good try. Let's see whether it works. What should be the value of
   new Trans(
    new CartesianPt(3,7),
    new Union(
    new Square(10),
    new Circle(10)))
  .*accept*(
    new UnionHasPt$^\mathcal{V}$(
    new CartesianPt(13,17)))?

So?

76   It provides the required methods: *forCircle*, *forSquare*, *forTrans*, and *forUnion*.

77   The first two additional words have an obvious meaning. They explicitly say that this visitor provides the services of UnionVisitor$^\mathcal{I}$. And, as we have said before, the addition of **public** is necessary, because this visitor **implements** an **interface**.

78   We know how *forTrans* works, so we're really asking whether
    new CartesianPt(10,10)
is inside the Union shape.

79   Which means that we're asking whether
    new CartesianPt(10,10)
is inside of
    new Square(10)
or inside of
    new Circle(10).

Okay. And what should be the answer?	[80] It should be **true**.

Let's see whether the value of
  new Trans(
    new CartesianPt(3,7),
    new Union(
      new Square(10),
      new Circle(10)))
  .*accept*(
    new UnionHasPt$^{\mathcal{V}}$(
      new CartesianPt(13,17)))
is true?
	[81] Usually we start by determining what kind of object we are working with.

And?	[82] It's a Shape$^{\mathcal{D}}$.

How did we construct this shape?	[83] With **Trans**.

Which method should we use on it?	[84] *forTrans*, of course.

Where is *forTrans* defined?	[85] It is defined in HasPt$^{\mathcal{V}}$.

So what should we do now?	[86] We should determine the value of
	    new Union(
	      new Square(10),
	      new Circle(10))
	    .*accept*(
	      new HasPt$^{\mathcal{V}}$(
	        new CartesianPt(10,10))).

What type of object is
  new Union(
    new Square(10),
    new Circle(10))?
	[87] It's a Shape$^{\mathcal{D}}$.

How did we construct this Shape$^{\mathcal{D}}$?	[88] With Union.

So which method should we use on it?	[89] *forUnion*, of course.

How do we find the appropriate *forUnion* method?	[90] In *accept*, which is defined in Union, we confirm that
	new HasPt$^{\mathcal{V}}$(
	new CartesianPt(10,10))
	is a UnionVisitor$^{\mathcal{I}}$ and then invoke its *forUnion*.

Is an instance of HasPt$^{\mathcal{V}}$ a UnionVisitor$^{\mathcal{I}}$?	[91] No!

Does it contain a method *forUnion*?	[92] No!

Then what is the value of	[93] It doesn't have a value. We are stuck.[1]
new Union(	
new Square(10),	
new Circle(10))	
.*accept*(	
new HasPt$^{\mathcal{V}}$(	
new CartesianPt(10,10)))?	

[1] A Java program raises a `RuntimeException`, indicating that the attempt to confirm the `UnionVisitorI`*ness* of the object failed. More specifically, we would see the following when running the program:
```
java.lang.ClassCastException:  UnionHasPtV
    at Union.accept(...java:...)
    at UnionHasPtV.forTrans(...java:...)
    at Trans.accept(...java:...).
```

What do we do next?	[94] Relax. Read a novel. Take a nap.

Which of those is best?	[95] You guessed it: whatever you did is best.

We should have prepared this extension in a better way.	[96] How could we have done that?

Here is the definition of HasPt$^\mathcal{V}$ that we should have provided if we wanted to extend it without making changes.

```
class HasPt^V implements ShapeVisitor^I {
  Point^D p;
  HasPt^V(Point^D _p) {
    p = _p; }
  ShapeVisitor^I newHasPt(Point^D p) {
    return new HasPt^V(p); }

  public boolean forCircle(int r) {
    return p.distanceToO() ≤ r; }
  public boolean forSquare(int s) {
    if^1 (p.x ≤ s)
      return (p.y ≤ s);
    else
      return false; }
  public
    boolean forTrans(Point^D q,Shape^D s) {
      return
        s.accept(newHasPt(p.minus(q))); }
}
```

How does this definition differ from the previous one?

In two ways. First, it contains a new method: *newHasPt*. Second, it uses the new method in place of **new** HasPt$^\mathcal{V}$ in *forTrans*.

Good. What does *newHasPt* produce?

A new ShapeVisitor$^\mathcal{I}$, as its interface implies.

And how does it produce that?

By constructing a **new** instance of HasPt$^\mathcal{V}$.

Is *newHasPt* like a constructor?

It is virtually indistinguishable from a constructor, which is why it is above the line that separates constructors from methods.

Does that mean the new definition of $HasPt^{\mathcal{V}}$ and the previous one are really the same?[1]

_____

[1] A functional programmer would say that newHasPt and HasPtV are η-equivalent.

101 They are mostly indistinguishable. Both *forTrans*es, the one in the previous and the one in the new definition of $HasPt^{\mathcal{V}}$, produce the same values when they consume the same values.

_____

Very well. But how does that help us with our problem?

102 That's not obvious.

_____

Can we override *newHasPt* when we extend $HasPt^{\mathcal{V}}$?

103 Yes, we can override any method that we wish to override.

_____

Let's override *newHasPt* in $UnionHasPt^{\mathcal{V}}$.

104 When we override it, we need to make sure it produces a $ShapeVisitor^{\mathcal{I}}$.

_____

That's true. Should it produce a $HasPt^{\mathcal{V}}$ or a $UnionHasPt^{\mathcal{V}}$?

105 The latter. Then *forTrans* in $HasPt^{\mathcal{V}}$ keeps producing a $UnionHasPt^{\mathcal{V}}$, if we start with a $UnionHasPt^{\mathcal{V}}$.

_____

Good answer. Should we repeat it?

106 Let's just reread it.

_____

The Ninth Bit of Advice

If a datatype may have to be extended, be forward looking and use a constructor-like (overridable) method so that visitors can be extended, too.

And that's exactly what we need. Revise the definition of UnionHasPt$^{\mathcal{V}}$.[1]

¹⁰⁷ Here it is.

```
class UnionHasPtᵛ
   extends HasPtᵛ
   implements UnionVisitorᴵ {
   UnionHasPtᵛ(Pointᴰ _p) {
   super(_p); }
   ShapeVisitorᴵ newHasPt(Pointᴰ p) {
   return new UnionHasPtᵛ(p); }

   public
     boolean forUnion(Shapeᴰ s,Shapeᴰ t) {
     if (s.accept(this))
        return true;
     else
        return t.accept(this); }
}
```

_____

[1] The is an instance of the *factory method* pattern [4].

If we assemble all this into one picture, what do we get?

¹⁰⁸ A drawing that helps our understanding of the relationships among the classes and interfaces.

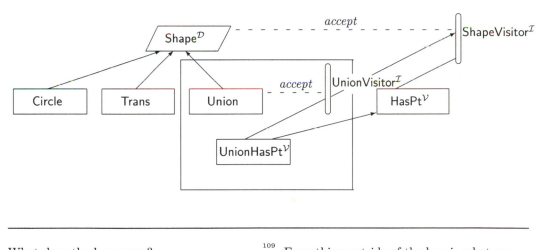

What does the box mean?

¹⁰⁹ Everything outside of the box is what we designed originally and considered to be unchangeable; everything inside is our extension.

Does the picture convey the key idea of this chapter?

110 No. It does not show the addition of a constructor-like method to HasPt$^{\mathcal{V}}$ and how it is overridden in UnionHasPt$^{\mathcal{V}}$.

Is anything missing?

111 Square, but that's okay.

Let's see whether this definition works. What is the value of
```
new Trans(
  new CartesianPt(3,7),
  new Union(
    new Square(10),
    new Circle(10)))
.accept(
  new UnionHasPt^V(
  new CartesianPt(13,17)))?
```

112 We remember that the shape was built with Trans.

Which method should we use on it?

113 *forTrans*, of course.

Where is *forTrans* defined?

114 It is defined in HasPt$^{\mathcal{V}}$.

So what should we do now?

115 We should determine the value of
```
new Union(
  new Square(10),
  new Circle(10))
.accept(
  this.newHasPt(
  new CartesianPt(10,10))).
```

What is **this**?

116 The current visitor, of course.

And how does that work?

117 We determine the value of
```
this.newHasPt(
  new CartesianPt(10,10))
```
and then use *accept* for the rest.

And what do we create?	[118] The new UnionVisitor$^\mathcal{I}$:
	  new UnionHasPt$^\mathcal{V}$(
	    new CartesianPt(10,10)).

What is the value of
  new Union(
    new Square(10),
    new Circle(10))
  .*accept*(
    new UnionHasPt$^\mathcal{V}$(
      new CartesianPt(10,10)))?
	[119] UnionHasPt$^\mathcal{V}$ also satisfies the interface ShapeVisitor$^\mathcal{I}$, so now we can invoke the *forUnion* method.

How do we do that?	[120] We first determine the value of
	  new Square(10)
	  .*accept*(
	    new UnionHasPt$^\mathcal{V}$(
	      new CartesianPt(10,10))).
	
	If it is **true**, we're done.

Is it **true**?	[121] It is. So we're done and we got the value we expected.
Are we happy now?	[122] Ecstatic.
Is it good to have extensible definitions?	[123] Yes. People should use extensible definitions if they want their code to be used more than once.
Very well. Does this mean we can put together flexible and extensible definitions if we use visitor protocols with these constructor-like methods?	[124] Yes, we can and should always do so.
And why is that?	[125] Because no program is ever finished.
Are you hungry yet?	[126] Are our meals ever finished?

10.
The State of
Things to Come

Have you ever wondered where the pizza pies come from?	[1] You should have, because someone needs to make the pie.

Here is our pizza pieman. Here is our pizza pieman.

[2] This is beyond anything we have seen before.

```
class Pieman^M implements Pieman^I {
  Pie^D p = new Bot();
  public int addTop(Object t) {
    p = new Top(t,p)
    ;
    return occTop(t); }
  public int remTop(Object t) {
    p = (Pie^D)p.accept(new Rem^V(t))
    ;
    return occTop(t); }
  public int substTop(Object n,Object o) {
    p = (Pie^D)p.accept(new Subst^V(n,o))
    ;
    return occTop(n); }
  public int occTop(Object o) {
    return
      ((Integer)p.accept(new Occurs^V(o)))
      .intValue(); }
}
```

$^{\mathcal{M}}$ This superscript is a reminder that the class manages a data structure. Lower superscripts when you enter this kind of definition in a file: PiemanM.

How so? Haven't we seen Pie$^{\mathcal{D}}$, Top, and Bot before?	[3] We have seen them.

And haven't we seen visitors like Rem$^{\mathcal{V}}$, Subst$^{\mathcal{V}}$, and Occurs$^{\mathcal{V}}$ for various datatypes?	[4] Yes, yes. But what are the stand-alone semicolons about?

Let's not worry about them for a while.	[5] Fine, but they are weird.

Here is the **interface** for Pieman$^\mathcal{M}$.

```
interface Pieman^I {
  int addTop(Object t);
  int remTop(Object t);
  int substTop(Object n,Object o);
  int occTop(Object o);
}
```

6 Isn't it missing p?

We don't specify fields in interfaces. And in any case, we don't want anybody else to see p.

7 Whatever.

Here are PieVisitor$^\mathcal{I}$ and Pie$^\mathcal{D}$.

```
interface PieVisitor^I {
  Object forBot();
  Object forTop(Object t,Pie^D r);
}
```

```
abstract class Pie^D {
  abstract
    Object accept(PieVisitor^I ask);
}
```

Define Bot and Top.

8 They are very familiar.

```
class Bot extends Pie^D {
  Object accept(PieVisitor^I ask) {
    return ask.forBot(); }
}
```

```
class Top extends Pie^D {
  Object t;
  Pie^D r;
  Top(Object _t,Pie^D _r) {
    t = _t;
    r = _r; }

  Object accept(PieVisitor^I ask) {
    return ask.forTop(t,r); }
}
```

Here is Occurs$^{\mathcal{V}}$. It counts how often some topping occurs on a pie.

```
class Occurs^V implements PieVisitor^I {
  Object a;
  Occurs^V(Object _a) {
    a = _a; }

  public Object forBot() {
    return new Integer(0); }
  public Object forTop(Object t,Pie^D r) {
    if (t.equals(a))
      return
        new Integer(((Integer)
                    (r.accept(this)))
                    .intValue()
                    + 1);
    else
      return r.accept(this); }
}
```

Great! Now we have almost all the visitors for our pieman. Define Rem$^{\mathcal{V}}$, which removes a topping from a pie.

9
And this little visitor substitutes one good topping for another.

```
class Subst^V implements PieVisitor^I {
  Object n;
  Object o;
  Subst^V(Object _n,Object _o) {
    n = _n;
    o = _o; }

  public Object forBot() {
    return new Bot(); }
  public Object forTop(Object t,Pie^D r) {
    if (o.equals(t))
      return
        new Top(n,(Pie^D)r.accept(this));
    else
      return
        new Top(t,(Pie^D)r.accept(this)); }
}
```

10
We remember that one, too.

```
class Rem^V implements PieVisitor^I {
  Object o;
  Rem^V(Object _o) {
    o = _o; }

  public Object forBot() {
    return new Bot(); }
  public Object forTop(Object t,Pie^D r) {
    if (o.equals(t))
      return r.accept(this);
    else
      return
        new Top(t,(Pie^D)r.accept(this)); }
}
```

Now we are ready to talk. What is the value of
$$\textbf{new } \text{Pieman}^{\mathcal{M}}().\mathit{occTop}(\textbf{new } \text{Anchovy}())?$$

11 We first create a Pieman$^{\mathcal{M}}$ and then ask how many anchovies occur on the pie.

Which pie?

12 The pie named p in the new Pieman$^{\mathcal{M}}$.

And how many anchovies are on that pie?

13 None.

And what is the value of
$$\textbf{new } \text{Pieman}^{\mathcal{M}}().\mathit{addTop}(\textbf{new } \text{Anchovy}())?$$

14 That's where those stand-alone semicolons come in again. They were never explained.

True. If we wish to determine the value of
$$\textbf{new } \text{Pieman}^{\mathcal{M}}().\mathit{addTop}(\textbf{new } \text{Anchovy}()),$$
we must understand what
$$p = \textbf{new } \text{Top}(\textbf{new } \text{Anchovy}(),p)$$
$$;$$
$$\textbf{return } \mathit{occTop}(\textbf{new } \text{Anchovy}())$$
means?

15 Yes, we must understand that. There is no number x in the world for which
$$x = x + 1,$$
so why should we expect there to be a Java p such that
$$p = \textbf{new } \text{Top}(\textbf{new } \text{Anchovy}(),p)?$$

That's right. But that's what happens when you have one too many double espressos.

16 So what does it mean?

Here it means that p changes and that future references to p reflect the change.

17 And the change is that p has a new topping, right?

When does the future begin?

18 Does it begin below the stand-alone semicolon?

That's precisely what a stand-alone semicolon means. Now do we know what
$$\textbf{return } \mathit{occTop}(\textbf{new } \text{Anchovy}())$$
produces?

19 It produces the number of anchovies on p.

And how many are there?	²⁰ We added one, so the value is 1.

And now what is the value of
$$\textbf{new Pieman}^{\mathcal{M}}().addTop(\textbf{new Anchovy}())?$$

²¹ It's 2, isn't it?

No, it's not. Take a close look. We created a **new** pieman, and that pieman added only one anchovy to his p.

²² Oh, isn't there a way to place several requests with the same pieman?

Yes, there is. Take a look at this:
$$\text{Pieman}^{\mathcal{I}} \ y = \textbf{new Pieman}^{\mathcal{M}}().$$

²³ Okay, y stands for some pieman.

What is the value of
$$y.addTop(\textbf{new Anchovy}())?$$

²⁴ 1. We know that.

And now what is the value of
$$y.substTop(\textbf{new Tuna}(),\textbf{new Anchovy}())?$$

²⁵ Still 1. According to the rules of semicolon and =, this replaces all anchovies on p with tunas, changes p, and then counts how many tunas are on p.

Correct. So what is the value of
$$y.occTop(\textbf{new Anchovy}())?$$

²⁶ 0, because y's pie no longer contains any anchovies.

Very good. And now take a look at this:
$$\text{Pieman}^{\mathcal{I}} \ yy = \textbf{new Pieman}^{\mathcal{M}}().$$
What is the value of
$$yy.addTop(\textbf{new Anchovy}())$$
$$;$$
$$yy.addTop(\textbf{new Anchovy}())$$
$$;$$
$$yy.addTop(\textbf{new Salmon}())$$
$$;$$
$$\ddots$$

²⁷ What are the
$$\ddots$$
doing at the end?

Because this is only half of what we want to look at. Here is the other half:

$yy.addTop(\textbf{new } \mathsf{Tuna}())$
;
$yy.addTop(\textbf{new } \mathsf{Tuna}())$
;
$yy.substTop(\textbf{new } \mathsf{Tuna}(),\textbf{new } \mathsf{Anchovy}())$?

28 4. First we add two anchovies, then a salmon, and two tunas. Then we substitute the two anchovies by two tunas. So yy's pie contains four tunas.

And what is the value of

$yy.remTop(\textbf{new } \mathsf{Tuna}())$

after we are through with all that?

29 It's 0, because $remTop$ first removes all tunas and then counts how many there are left.

Does that mean $remTop$ always produces 0?

30 Yes, it always does.

Now what is the value of

$yy.occTop(\textbf{new } \mathsf{Salmon}())$?

31 1.

And how about

$y.occTop(\textbf{new } \mathsf{Salmon}())$?

32 0, because y and yy are two different piemen.

Is yy the same pieman as before?

33 No, it changed.

So is it the same one?

34 When we eat a pizza pie, we change, but we are still the same.

When we asked yy to substitute all anchovies by tunas, did the pie change?

35 The p in yy changed, nothing else.

Does that mean that anybody can write

$yy.p = \textbf{new } \mathsf{Bot}()$

and thus change a pieman like yy?

36 No, because yy's type is $\mathsf{Pieman}^{\mathcal{I}}$, p isn't available. Only $addTop$, $remTop$, $substTop$, and $occTop$ are visible.

Isn't it good that we didn't include p in Pieman$^{\mathcal{I}}$?	37 Yes, with this trick we can prevent others from changing p (or parts of p) in strange ways. Everything is clear now.

Clear like soup?	38 Just like chicken soup.

Can we define a different version of Subst$^{\mathcal{V}}$ so that it changes toppings the way a pieman changes his pies?	39 We can't do that yet.

And that's what we discuss next. Do you need a break?	40 No, a cup of coffee will do.

41 Compare this new PieVisitor$^{\mathcal{I}}$ with the first one in this chapter.

```
interface PieVisitor$^{\mathcal{I}}$ {
  Object forBot(Bot that);
  Object forTop(Top that);
}
```

It isn't all that different. A PieVisitor$^{\mathcal{I}}$ must still provide two methods: *forBot* and *forTop*, except that the former now consumes a Bot and the latter a Top.

42 True. Here is the unchanged datatype.

```
abstract class Pie$^{\mathcal{D}}$ {
  abstract
    Object accept(PieVisitor$^{\mathcal{I}}$ ask);
}
```

Define the Bot variant.

The definition is straightforward.

```
class Bot extends Pie$^{\mathcal{D}}$ {
  Object accept(PieVisitor$^{\mathcal{I}}$ ask) {
    return ask.forBot(this); }
}
```

43 Is it? Why does it use **this**?

We only have one instance of Bot when we use *forBot*, namely **this**, so *forBot* is clearly supposed to consume **this**.

That's progress. And that's what happens in
Top, too.

44
Interesting.

```
class Top extends Pie^D {
  Object t;
  Pie^D r;
  Top(Object _t,Pie^D _r) {
    t = _t;
    r = _r; }

  Object accept(PieVisitor^I ask) {
    return ask.forTop(this); }
}
```

Modify this version of Occurs^V so that it **implements** the new PieVisitor^I.

45
The *forBot* method basically stays the same, but *forTop* changes somewhat.

```
class Occurs^V implements PieVisitor^I {
  Object a;
  Occurs^V(Object _a) {
    a = _a; }

  public Object forBot() {
    return new Integer(0); }
  public Object forTop(Object t,Pie^D r) {
    if (t.equals(a))
      return
        new Integer(((Integer)
                    (r.accept(this)))
                    .intValue()
                    + 1);
    else
      return r.accept(this); }
}
```

```
class Occurs^V implements PieVisitor^I {
  Object a;
  Occurs^V(Object _a) {
    a = _a; }

  public Object forBot(Bot that) {
    return new Integer(0); }
  public Object forTop(Top that) {
    if (that.t.equals(a))
      return
        new Integer(((Integer)
                    (that.r.accept(this)))
                    .intValue()
                    + 1);
    else
      return that.r.accept(this); }
}
```

How does *forBot* change?

46
It now consumes a Bot, which is why we had to add (Bot *that*) behind its name.

How does *forTop* change?	[47] It no longer receives the field values of the corresponding Top. Instead it consumes the entire object, which makes the two fields available as *that.t* and *that.r*.
And?	[48] With that, we can replace the fields t and r with *that.t* and *that.r*.
Isn't that easy?	[49] This modification of Occurs$^{\mathcal{V}}$ certainly is.
Then try Rem$^{\mathcal{V}}$.	[50] It's easy; we use the same trick.

```
class Rem^V implements PieVisitor^I {
  Object o;
  Rem^V(Object _o) {
    o = _o; }

  public Object forBot(Bot that) {
    return new Bot(); }
  public Object forTop(Top that) {
    if (o.equals(that.t))
      return that.r.accept(this);
    else
      return
        new Top(that.t,
          (Pie^D)that.r.accept(this)); }
}
```

Do we need to do Subst$^{\mathcal{V}}$?	[51] Not really. It should be just like Rem$^{\mathcal{V}}$.
And indeed, it is. Happy now?	[52] So far, so good. But what's the point of this exercise?
Oh, Point$^{\mathcal{D}}$s? They will show up later.	[53] Seriously.

Here is the point. What is new about this version of Subst$^{\mathcal{V}}$?

```
class Subst𝒱 implements PieVisitor𝓘 {
  Object n;
  Object o;
  Subst𝒱(Object _n,Object _o) {
    n = _n;
    o = _o; }

  public Object forBot(Bot that) {
    return that; }
  public Object forTop(Top that) {
    if (o.equals(that.t)) {
      that.t = n
      ;
      that.r.accept(this)
      ;
      return that; }
    else {
      that.r.accept(this)
      ;
      return that; }
  }
}
```

54 There are no **news**.

Don't they say "no **news** is good news?"

55 Does this saying apply here, too?

Yes, because we want to define a version of Subst$^{\mathcal{V}}$ that modifies toppings without constructing a **new** pie.

56 That's a way of putting it.

What do the methods of Subst$^{\mathcal{V}}$ always **return**?

57 They always return *that*, which is the object that they consume.

So how do they substitute toppings?

58 By changing the *that* before they return it. Specifically, they change the *t* field of *that* to *n* when it equals *o*.

What?

$$\mathit{that.t = n}$$

does it.

Correct. And from here on, *that.t* holds the new topping. What is

$$\mathit{that.r.accept}(\mathbf{this})$$

about?

In the previous Subst$^\mathcal{V}$, *r.accept*(**this**) created a **new** pie from *r* with all toppings appropriately substituted. In our new version, *that.r.accept*(**this**) modifies the pie *r* so that below the following semicolon it contains the appropriate toppings.

Is there anything else to say about the new Subst$^\mathcal{V}$?

Not really. It does what it does, which is what we wanted.[1]

---
[1] This is a true instance of the *visitor* pattern [4]. What we previously called "visitor" pattern instances, were simple variations on the theme.

Do we have to change Pieman$^\mathcal{M}$?

No, we didn't change what the visitors do, we only changed how they do things.

Is it truly safe to modify the toppings of a pie?

Yes, because the Pieman$^\mathcal{M}$ manages the toppings of *p*, and nobody else sees *p*.

Can we do LtdSubst$^\mathcal{V}$ now without creating new instances of LtdSubst$^\mathcal{V}$ or Top?

Now that's a piece of pie.

The Tenth Bit of Advice

When modifications to objects are needed, use a class to insulate the operations that modify objects. Otherwise, beware the consequences of your actions.

Here is a true dessert. It will help us understand what the point of state is.

```
abstract class Point^D {
  int x;
  int y;
  Point^D(int _x,int _y) {
    x = _x;
    y = _y; }
─────────────────────────────
  boolean closerToO(Point^D p) {
    return
      distanceToO() ≤ p.distanceToO(); }
  Point^D minus(Point^D p) {
    return
      new CartesianPt(x − p.x,y − p.y); }
  abstract int distanceToO();
}
```

65 The datatype has three extensions.

```
class CartesianPt extends Point^D {
  CartesianPt(int _x,int _y) {
    super(_x,_y); }
─────────────────────────────
  int distanceToO() {
    return ⌊√(x² + y²)⌋; }
}
```

$$\text{return } \lfloor\sqrt{x^2 + y^2}\rfloor; \}$$

```
class ManhattanPt extends Point^D {
  ManhattanPt(int _x,int _y) {
    super(_x,_y); }
─────────────────────────────
  int distanceToO() {
    return x + y; }
}
```

```
class ShadowedManhattanPt
    extends ManhattanPt {
  int Δ_x;
  int Δ_y;
  ShadowedManhattanPt(int _x,
                      int _y,
                      int _Δ_x,
                      int _Δ_y) {
    super(_x,_y);
    Δ_x = _Δ_x;
    Δ_y = _Δ_y; }
─────────────────────────────
  int distanceToO() {
    return
      super.distanceToO()+Δ_x + Δ_y; }
}
```

Aren't we missing a variant?

66 Yes, we are missing ShadowedCartesianPt.

Good enough. We won't need it. Here is one point:

    new ManhattanPt(1,4).

If this point represents a child walking down the streets of Manhattan, how do we represent his movement?

67

Shouldn't we add a method that changes all the fields of the points?

Yes. Add to Point$^\mathcal{D}$ the method *moveBy*, which consumes two **int**s and changes the fields of a point appropriately.

68

First we must know what the method is supposed to produce.

The method should return the new distance to the origin.

69

Now we know how to do this.

```
abstract class Point𝒟 {
  int x;¹
  int y;
  Point𝒟(int _x,int _y) {
    x = _x;
    y = _y; }

  boolean closerToO(Point𝒟 p) {
    return
      distanceToO() ≤ p.distanceToO(); }
  Point𝒟 minus(Point𝒟 p) {
    return
      new CartesianPt(x − p.x,y − p.y); }
  int moveBy(int Δx,int Δy) {
    x = x + Δx
    ;
    y = y + Δy
    ;
    return distanceToO(); }
  abstract int distanceToO();
}
```

Let *ptChild* stand for

    new ManhattanPt(1,4).

What is the value of

    ptChild.distanceToO()?

70

5.

What is the value of *ptChild.moveBy*(2,8)?	[71] 15.

Good. Now let's watch a child with a
helium-filled balloon that casts a shadow.
Let *ptChildBalloon* be
   new ShadowedManhattanPt(1,4,1,1).
What is the value of
   ptChildBalloon.distanceToO()?
	[72] 7.

What is the value of *ptChildBalloon.moveBy*(2,8)?	[73] 17, of course.

Did the balloon move, too?	[74] Yes, it just moved along as we moved the point.

Isn't that powerful?	[75] It sure is. We added one method, used it, and everything moved.

The more things change, the cheaper our desserts get.	[76] Yes, but to get to the dessert, we had to work quite hard.

Correct but now we are through and it is time to go out and to celebrate with a grand dinner.	[77] Don't forget to leave a tip.

Commencement

You have reached the end of your introduction to computation with classes, interfaces, and objects. Are you now ready to tackle a major programming problem? Programming requires two kinds of knowledge: understanding the nature of computation, and discovering the lexicon, features, and idiosyncrasies of a particular programming language. The first of these is the more difficult intellectual task. If you understand the material in this book, you have mastered that challenge. Still, it would be well worth your time to develop a fuller understanding of all the capabilities in Java—this requires getting access to a running Java system and mastering those idiosyncrasies. If you want to understand Java and object-oriented systems in greater depth, take a look at the following books:

References

1. Arnold and Gosling. *The Java Programming Language.* Addison-Wesley, Reading, Massachusetts, 1996.

2. Buschmann, Meunier, Rohnert, Sommerlad, and Stal. *A System of Patterns: Pattern-Oriented Software Architecture.* John Wiley & Sons, Ltd. Chichester, Europe, 1996.

3. Firesmith and Eykholt. *Dictionary of Object Technology.* SIGS Books, Inc., New York, New York, 1995 and Prentice Hall, Englewood Cliffs, New Jersey, 1995.

4. Gamma, Helm, Johnson, and Vlissides. *Design Patterns.* Addison-Wesley, Reading, Massachusetts, 1994.

5. Gosling, Joy, and Steele. *The Java Language Specification.* Addison-Wesley, Reading, Massachusetts, 1996.

6. Pree. *Design Patterns for Object-Oriented Software Development.* Addison-Wesley, Reading, Massachusetts, 1994.

Index

This is for the loyal Schemers and MLers.

No, we wouldn't forget factorial.

```
interface T^I {
  o→o^I apply(T^I x);
}
```

```
interface o→o^I {
  Object apply(Object x);
}
```

```
interface oo→oo^I {
  o→o^I apply(o→o^I x);
}
```

```
interface oo→oo→oo^I {
  o→o^I apply(oo→oo^I x);
}
```

```
class Y implements oo→oo→oo^I {
  public o→o^I apply(oo→oo^I f) {
    return new H(f).apply(new H(f)); }
}
```

```
class H implements T^I {
  oo→oo^I f;
  H(oo→oo^I _f) {
    f = _f; }
  public o→o^I apply(T^I x) {
    return f.apply(new G(x)); }
}
```

```
class G implements o→o^I {
  T^I x;
  G(T^I _x) {
    x = _x; }
  public Object apply(Object y) {
    return (x.apply(x)).apply(y); }
}
```

```
class MkFact implements oo→oo^I {
  public o→o^I apply(o→o^I fact) {
    return new Fact(fact); }
}
```

```
class Fact implements o→o^I {
  o→o^I fact;
  Fact(o→o^I _fact) {
    fact = _fact; }
  public Object apply(Object i) {
    int inti = ((Integer)i).intValue();
    if (inti == 0)
      return new Integer(1);
    else
      return
        new Integer(
          inti
          *
          ((Integer)
           fact.apply(new Integer(inti − 1)))
          .intValue()); }
}
```